Britain and the
European Union

382·9142·

Books in the Politics Study Guides series

British Government and Politics: A Comparative Guide
Duncan Watts

International Politics: An Introductory Guide
Alasdair Blair, Steven Curtis and Sean McGough

US Government and Politics
William Storey

Britain and the European Union
Alistair Jones

The Changing Constitution
Kevin Harrison and Tony Boyd

Democracy in Britain
Matt Cole

Devolution in the United Kingdom
Russell Deacon and Alan Sandry

Elections and Voting in Britain
Chris Robinson

The Judiciary, Civil Liberties and Human Rights
Steven Foster

Political Communication
Steven Foster

Political Parties in Britain
Matt Cole

The Politics of Northern Ireland
Joanne McEvoy

Pressure Groups
Duncan Watts

The Prime Minister and Cabinet
Stephen Buckley

The UK Parliament
Moyra Grant

Britain and the European Union

Alistair Jones

Edinburgh University Press

© Alistair Jones, 2007

Edinburgh University Press Ltd
22 George Square, Edinburgh

Typeset in 11/13pt Monotype Baskerville by
Servis Filmsetting Ltd, Manchester, and
printed and bound in Spain by
GraphyCems

A CIP record for this book is available from the British Library

ISBN 978 0 7486 2428 7 (paperback)

The right of Alistair Jones to be identified as author of this work
has been asserted in accordance with the Copyright, Designs and
Patents Act 1988.

Contents

Boxes

Tables

Acknowledgements

There is a number of people to whom I must extend my thanks for their support while writing this book. First among these is my wife, Claire, who has been full of encouragement, urging me to finish the book. She also provided numerous valuable comments on earlier manuscripts.

I must also thank colleagues at De Montfort University for their support. In particular, I thank Professor John Greenwood, Clive Gray and Alison Statham, as well as all the staff in the Department of Public Policy.

Thanks must also be extended to Professor Martin Holland, Director of the National Centre for Research on Europe at the University of Canterbury in New Zealand, who first sparked my interest in the then European Community when I was an undergraduate student.

I would also like to thank the series editor, Duncan Watts, who provided a range of valuable comments on earlier drafts. I must also thank Nicola Ramsey and James Dale at Edinburgh University Press for their support.

Finally, I must thank the cats (Nua and Sasha) and dogs (Max and Tiny) for reminding me that walking, feeding, and playing with them were not, under any circumstances, distractions from writing.

As ever, if there are any errors or omissions in this text, the fault lies entirely with me.

Introduction

Contents

Overview

The relationship between Britain and the European Union is phenomenally complex. There appear to be inconsistencies in the attitudes of the British government, the British media and the British people towards the European Union – and vice versa. The label for Britain that is often bandied around when describing the relationship is 'reluctant European'. Throughout this book, we shall return again and again to this theme. The basic problem is that a specific definition or explanation of the concept often eludes most people. Such an inconsistency fits in well with Britain's overall relationship with the European Union, however. As with terms such as 'pro-European' or 'Euro-sceptic', 'reluctant European' can be twisted and contorted to fit whatever issue is being examined. This chapter is going to introduce some of these themes, which are then addressed throughout the book.

Key issues to be covered in this chapter

- An introduction and an overview to this book
- An outline of the key terms and concepts
- Issues and concerns which will be addressed in the book

Introduction

The way in which Britain's relationship with the European Union (EU) is portrayed in much of the British media is such that many people seem to be of the opinion that Britain is not even a member of the Union. Membership of the European Union, it seems, is to be avoided at all costs. Britain has a long history and tradition of looking far beyond Europe to the rest of the world – there is the Commonwealth (formerly the British Empire) as well as the **special relationship** with the United States. These are seen to be of far greater importance. Yet, in the early post-war years, Winston Churchill described the Western world's defence against communism as being dependent upon three concentric circles: the United States, the Empire, and Europe. Where these three circles intersected, that was Britain. Britain had a 'special relationship' with the United States; the British Empire covered a third of the world; and Britain was the strongest European power, having won World War II. Of the three concentric circles, the United States and the Empire were seen to be of far greater importance than the relationship with Europe – and, of course, English was spoken in most of these places! Europe, by comparison, was almost inconsequential. Britain was a global power that had stood up single-handedly against the tyranny of Hitler and the Nazis. Britain would never be dragged down to the European level. The fact that on 1 January 1973, Britain joined what was then known as the European Economic Community (EEC) – and sometimes described as the Common Market – is often conveniently overlooked. After all, there is the perception that, when fog appears in the English Channel, it cuts off Europe from Britain, not vice versa.

What is also disheartening about these attitudes is that very few people appear willing to stand up and contest them. It is possible to refute the importance of the 'special relationship' and of the role of the Commonwealth. For example, the so-called 'special relationship' is not exactly a two-way one. It seems to be far more a case of Britain standing up to express support for whatever US policies are being condemned by other countries. Caricatures of Tony Blair have presented him as George W. Bush's poodle.

When turning to the Commonwealth, Britain is merely one member of the organisation. There is no longer a British dominance of the Commonwealth – if there ever was since its formation.

Politically and economically Britain is now a regional power, and the region to which Britain belongs is Europe. The problem is to convince people that this is the case. None of this really presents the case as to why the European Union is so important for Britain or why British membership is so important to the Union. At best, it highlights that the other options are flawed, but then so is the European option. The case for Europe needs to be presented, but presented even-handedly. Portraying the relationship through rose-tinted spectacles is likely to do more harm than good.

The intention within this book is to try to raise the profile of the European Union in the United Kingdom and vice versa. There are many benefits – and problems – resulting from British membership of the EU. Only the negative aspects appear to gain publicity, however. Similarly, the European Union has benefited from British membership, but all that tends to be bandied around is that Britain is a **reluctant European** and that the British are not committed to the European project. The reasons for such negativity include the fact that people are ill-informed about the relationship between Britain

---

Box 1.1 A perspective on UK–EU relations

'Britain's relationship with the European Community can be summed up as follows. The government lacks any sense of purpose about Britain's role in Europe, and consequently its policies are riddled with contradiction and ambiguity. Any initiative that might result in Britain becoming more deeply involved in European institutions brings these inconsistencies to the surface, with the government then moving into a state of disarray accompanied by bitter party conflict and occasional resignations. There are those who put their Europeanism above party loyalty whilst others, including the Prime Minister, seem prepared to sacrifice Europe for any short-term party political advantage. The Prime Minister's position on the EC issue has invited challenges from political rivals for the key to No. 10. For many, fundamental hostility towards the EC masquerades as arguments about the sovereignty of Parliament, about alien ideologies being thrust upon Britain by the unelected bureaucrats of Brussels or about the undesirable national characteristics of our partners, particularly the French and Germans . . .

This state of affairs, of course, refers to the last days of the Wilson government . . .'[1]

and the EU, as well as what sometimes appears to be deliberate attempts to damage the relationship.

The approach taken in this book will be, firstly, to examine the historical development of the European Union. This will be followed by an evaluation of the institutions and the common policies of the EU. Thereafter, the focus moves specifically to the relationship between Britain and the Union – how each influences the other. The roles of political parties and public opinion are examined later in the book. Prior to this, some theoretical concepts are assessed. Terms, such as supranationalism and integration, are defined, and then the British position on each is evaluated. Thus, in the concluding chapter, it will be possible to assess the extent to which Britain is still a reluctant European.

At the end of each chapter, there is a summary of key points. As well as this, there are definitions of important terms that were used in that chapter. There are also lists of useful websites and supplementary readings. These can be used to access primary sources of material to enable readers to formulate their own opinions on the various aspects of this book.

Content of the book

The history and development of the European Union, which are examined in chapter 2, saw a lack of British involvement until the 1970s, and this contributed to Britain earning the label 'reluctant European'. Yet this lack of participation in the European Coal and Steel Community (ECSC) and in the European Economic Community (EEC) did not mean that Britain failed to influence their development. British actions outside both these organisations – particularly in the formation of the European Free Trade Association (EFTA) – had an impact upon them. Added to this, Britain participated in other European ventures such as the European Defence Community. While such an organisation was outside the ambit of the ECSC, British willingness to participate highlighted a degree of commitment towards Europe that has really gone unreported. Thus the label 'reluctant European' may actually have been applicable to certain aspects of Britain's relationship with Europe.

Yet, even after joining the then European Economic Community, the label 'reluctant European' did not go away. This was despite full participation in all the institutions of the EEC – as can be seen in chapter 3. There was no empty chair presidency from the British – as the French had in the mid-1960s.

The label did seem to be warranted over some of the common policies of the EEC and EU, however. Successive British governments have been anything but enthusiastic about the Common Agricultural Policy (CAP), as well as some of the other common policies and the development of the single currency, the euro. Britain has long argued for reform of the CAP and other policies, as is detailed in chapter 4. British governments have also negotiated opt-outs of particular policies, such as the euro and the social charter. While the British are castigated for doing so, it should be noted that other member states, such as Sweden and Denmark, have also negotiated opt-outs over joining the euro. And when it comes to reform of common policies, Britain is often to the forefront in the fight against the more reactionary, conservative member states. Yet the fight for reform is often presented as Britain attempting to change long-established policies, to make Europe operate in a manner closer to that of the United States – particularly with regard to issues such as employment law. Thus, Britain is presented as not being committed to the European social-democratic economic model but rather to the American free market, *laissez-faire* model where the rights and freedoms of the individual are crushed beneath the corporate animal of big business.

So, while some Europeans are not enthusiastic about British membership, and many Britons appear unenthusiastic about EU membership, what is interesting is the extent to which each has had a positive impact upon the other. Britain's role in trying to modernise the European Union has already been noted above. Yet the EU has had a huge impact – and more often than not an unreported impact – upon Britain. While this impact is assessed in chapter 5, it is important to note here that the impact of the European Union in Britain has both positive and negative aspects. Negative aspects include the increase in bureaucracy or 'red tape' that has resulted through membership. Yet much of the reason for this is the more legalistic approach of other EU member states towards issues such as regulation. In Britain in the past, much regulation was done through a 'hands off' approach where one simply trusted some one's word. If you could not trust a chap's word, what could you trust? As a result of this approach, much regulation in Britain was carried out ineffectively. The more legalistic approach, adopted by the other EU member states, provided far greater information and protection for people. Britain has been compelled to step into line in areas such as health and safety. As a result, the regulation seems to be more effective. The downside of this is that it is a slow, bureaucratic process.

Where Europe has had an important impact upon Britain is at the level of subnational government. Although Britain is still considered to be a unitary and heavily centralised state, with all power focused upon its parliament, membership of the European Union has enabled regional and local government to develop some roles without having excessive interference from the centre. The current Blair government has pushed this along by holding successful referendums in Scotland, Wales, Northern Ireland and London for forms of devolution. These devolved bodies are able to participate within the EU through such bodies as the Committee of Regions. Pre-1997, such participation would have been considered to be a pipe dream.

Britain also has a key role to play in the future development of the European Union. Issues such as the extent to which the EU moves further down a **supranationalist** or **integrationist** route are examined in chapters 6 and 7. Britain's role here can be pivotal. As one of the four largest member states, Britain has the opportunity to influence the integrationist agenda. Which other powers, if any, could (or should) be ceded to Brussels? Alternatively, via subsidiarity, which powers could (or should) be returned to member states? Similarly, with expansion of the Union, Britain will play an important role in any future enlargement of it. While a unanimous decision is required to support any enlargement, Britain has played a key role in brokering deals. Most recently, the Turkish application for membership was kept on track by British action. Smaller countries (such as Portugal), which carry less weight or influence in the Council of Ministers, are often happy to see Britain stand up and fight for a particular issue. If it were left to the smaller countries, there would be a high probability that their opinions would be crushed under the juggernaut of the larger member states.

Yet all of this seems to presuppose that there is a consistent British position within the European Union. This is not the case. Even within individual political parties in Britain, there is no uniform position. As will be seen in chapter 8, each of the major British political parties is divided over the issue of Europe. The Conservative, Labour and the Liberal Democratic parties each has representatives who are enthusiastic about the European Union, but also those who are more likely to desire British withdrawal from it. Most MPs seem willing to toe the line of their party leadership, but even the leaders change their opinions about Europe. Thus, it becomes very difficult for the public to get any sort of prompt from the political parties on the issue of Europe.

It is to public opinion on Europe that we turn in chapter 9. This chapter goes beyond just British public opinion. It will also focus upon public opinion in other member states. The British public is often presented as being ill-informed or even uninformed on EU issues, but the reality is that it is not the only one. It has been suggested that the 'No' votes for the EU constitution returned in referendums in France and the Netherlands have been, in part, attributed to a lack of knowledge as to what the Union is all about!

In the final chapter, we return to the question of the 'reluctant European'. Specifically, it is about the extent to which Britain may still be considered worthy of such a label. As noted earlier, the problem is over the definition. With a clear definition, it would be easy to assess the extent to which Britain is still the 'reluctant European'. The problem is that there is more than one definition, and utilising different definitions gives different results. Sitting on the fence and saying 'Maybe' does not address the issue either. Yet, wariness in casting the label may be the way forward. Britain might be a 'reluctant European' in certain policy areas, but not so in others. Possibly the label ought to be the 'cautious European'.

Because Britain did not join the euro, it could be argued that it is a 'reluctant European'. Yet joining the euro has not been ruled out. Gordon Brown, the Chancellor of the Exchequer, has laid out specific criteria that have to be met before he feels that Britain could join the euro. His five economic tests have been laid out so as to make sure that the British economy can cope with the changes involved – but also so that the European economy can cope with the impact of British membership. Clearly, this is the sign of a 'cautious European'.

Those of a more cynical persuasion might argue, however, that the five economic tests can not be met, that they are too artificial, and that the reality is that the Chancellor does not want Britain to join the euro under his watch. As it stands, should the five tests be met, there is a commitment to hold a referendum on joining the euro. No prime minister (or chancellor of the exchequer) would want to hold a referendum that they are likely to lose. Thus, there is a line of argument which says that the five economic tests will be met only once it seems likely that the British public will support joining the euro.

There is a similar line of argument over the draft EU Constitution. The Blair government committed itself to holding a referendum on the constitution. With the French and Dutch having already returned 'No' votes, no moves have been made in Britain to hold a referendum. Eurosceptics want the referendum to be held simply to make sure that it is not resurrected in another guise, but also as it is likely that the British public would not support the EU constitution anyway. As with the Euro referendum, however, it is unlikely that it will be held in Britain unless the 'right' result is likely to be achieved. Is this the action (or lack thereof) of a 'cautious European' or a reluctant one?

....

✅ What you should have learnt from reading this chapter

- There is a debate over what a 'reluctant European' is.

- In the United Kingdom, the negative aspects of the European Union tend to be highlighted far more frequently than the positive ones.

- There are different ways of interpreting key terms and concepts.

🔍 Glossary of key terms

Integration The idea here is of combining a range of different pieces into a single body. Within the context of the European Union, this is where the different member states move closer and closer together, and may eventually become one.

Reluctant European This is a phrase used to describe the lack of British commitment to the European Union. Britain was considered a reluctant European by not joining the original European Coal and Steel Community when it was formed. When Britain did eventually join, the label remained because Britain did not appear to be committed to developing the European project. It is a little surprising that only Britain appears worthy of such a label.

Special relationship A phrase used to describe the importance of the relationship between Britain and the United States. From a British perspective, it highlights that Britain, and British opinions, are considered to be of great importance to the most powerful country on Earth.

Supranationalism Such an approach sees countries working closely together. They cede sovereignty in certain areas to a higher authority which will co-ordinate and police the making and implementation of policies in those specified areas across the organisation.

Likely examination questions

Why does Britain's relationship with the European Union seem so complex?

'Britain always looks across the pond to the United States rather than across the ditch to Europe.' Evaluate the accuracy of such a statement.

Helpful websites

One of the best places to obtain information about the EU is its own websites. There are many of them, but a useful starting point is europa.eu.int . For a positive perspective on British membership, look at the Foreign and Commonwealth Office website at www.fco.gov.uk. A more negative slant is given by the Campaign for an Independent Britain at www.bullen.demon.co.uk/index.htm.

Suggestions for further reading

There are many text books on the European Union. The best of these are M. Cini (ed.), *European Union Politics* (Oxford University Press, 2003); and N. Nugent, *The Government and Politics of the European Union* (Palgrave, 5th edition, 2002). For Britain's relationship with the EU, see D. Watts and C. Pilkington, *Britain in the EU Today* (Manchester University Press, 3rd edition, 2005). A slightly older historical perspective is given in L. Robins, 'Britain and the European Community: Twenty Years of Not Knowing' in B. Jones and L. Robins (eds), *Two Decades in British Politics* (Manchester University Press, 1992) pp. 243–55.

CHAPTER 2

History and Development of the European Union

Contents

Overview

The European Union has developed gradually from a collection of states pooling their coal and steel resources through to the more integrated union that exists today. This process has been anything but smooth. National interests have conflicted with Community aims and objectives. The various periods of enlargement have also changed the EU, from a group of six countries working fairly closely together to a rather unwieldy twenty-five member states that exist today. In this chapter, we examine the origins and the development of the organisation since World War II. The role of the United Kingdom is very important, both as a non-participant in the early years, and as an apparent 'reluctant European' ever since joining. The outside interests, particularly those of Britain, have also influenced how the European Union developed. The historical overview presented in this chapter is essential for a clear understanding of the institutions and common policies of the EU which are analysed in subsequent chapters.

Key issues to be covered in this chapter

- Origins and development of the European Coal and Steel Community
- Development of the EEC
- From EC to EU
- Britain's non-participation
- Enlargement
- The 'reluctant European'

The origins of the European Coal and Steel Community

The origins of the **European Coal and Steel Community (ECSC)** can be seen not just in the ruins of World War II but really from the aftermath of World War I. The fear of repeating the same mistakes, leading to the rise of fascism in Europe, haunted many politicians. Added to this was the fear of the growth of the communist regimes in Eastern Europe and the threat which they seemed to pose to life and liberty in Western Europe. Mix into this the memories of two world wars fought across the European continent, and the carnage left in their aftermath. Nobody wished to endure such devastation again.

The question was where to start in the rebuilding of Europe in the aftermath of World War II? Apart from the American money being pumped into Europe (or more specifically Western Europe) via the Marshall Plan, there was a feeling that Europe really needed to help itself. The basis of any such reconstruction of Europe required Franco-German reconciliation. The person credited with planning this reconciliation through intertwining the resources of heavy industry was **Jean Monnet**.

Monnet was not a politician. He was a bureaucrat. He developed a plan to integrate the French and German economies, however. He passed it on to the French Prime Minister, René Plevin, and to the French Foreign Secretary, Robert Schuman. It was Schuman who gave the political weight to Monnet's proposals, and thus there was the Schuman Plan.

Before anything could be started, Schuman required the support of the Americans and the West Germans. Konrad Adenauer, the West German chancellor, was very enthusiastic over the proposals, realising that it was a way in which the rehabilitation of West Germany on the international scene could be hastened. The pooling of **sovereignties** over the coal and steel resources was pivotal. American support was lukewarm at first but soon grew.

The next question for the French and West Germans was over which other countries shoud be invited into the 'club'. Eastern Europe was under Soviet domination and would not be asked. Many other countries, particularly those in northern Europe, treasured their neutrality and feared upsetting the Soviet Union, not to mention their reservations over **supranationalism**. Other countries were under the control of military regimes. This, in effect, left the Benelux countries (Belgium, the Netherlands and Luxembourg), Italy and the United Kingdom. The British response was dismissive. The view from London was that Britain was one of the world's leading powers, with a global empire. Added to this, its **'special relationship'** with the United States was far more important. At best, Britain saw itself as a bridge between the United States and continental Europe. Mere trifles in the continental backyard were not to be entertained. Besides, in the aftermath of World War II, Britain had only just nationalised its coal and steel industries. Having done this, there was no way in which it was willing then to 'surrender' its sovereignty to a supranational organisation.

The ECSC was established by the Treaty of Paris which was signed in April 1951. Six countries signed up to the organisation – Belgium, France, Italy, Luxembourg, the Netherlands and West Germany. A number of institutions was established, including the High Authority, an assembly, a council of ministers and a court of justice. Its headquarters was in Luxembourg, and the first president was Monnet. The ECSC began operating from August 1952.

This was a significant first for sovereign states – the idea of ceding aspects of national sovereignty to a supranational body. The ECSC could, among other things, adjust tariff barriers, abolish subsidies and fix prices. There was some national resistance but the integration of Belgium, Luxembourg and the Netherlands made the process much easier. The aim of creating a single market for coal and steel was not achieved but significant steps were taken in this area. It gave some impetus to developing the ECSC into a more diverse body – an economic community rather than dealing with specific aspects of national economies.

With the relative success of the ECSC came the aim of creating the **European Defence Community (EDC)**. This was a far more ambitious plan to promote co-operation on defence matters while incorporating West Germany into Western European defences. A draft treaty was drawn up in 1952 but was never ratified. A key reason for the failure to ratify was French nervousness over (West) German rearmament along with their reluctance to surrender control over their armed forces to a supranational organisation. Even today, there is still reluctance from a number of member states regarding the European Rapid Reaction Force.

From ECSC to EEC

The original idea from Monnet and Schuman was that the ECSC would develop slowly. It would be a long process of economic integration. The Benelux countries saw the potential to develop the ECSC far more quickly, however. They envisaged a full customs union, based on what already existed among themselves, but broadened to include all six ECSC members, together with any others who wished to join. At the Messina Conference in 1955, a committee was established, headed by the Belgian Foreign Minister, Paul-Henri Spaak, to investigate such a development. Spaak's proposals included the creation of a common market, greater integration of national economies, the development of common social policies, and the need to work together in developing some sort of common approach to atomic energy. The Spaak Report became the basis for the Treaty of Rome, the founding document of the **European Economic Community (EEC)** and the **European Atomic Agency (Euratom)**. The treaty was signed in March 1957 and came into force on 1 January 1958.

As with the formation of the ECSC, Britain was invited to participate. At the Messina Conference, the British government sent junior Foreign Office officials in an observer capacity. A number of committees was established by the British government to examine the consequences of the formation of the EEC. One of their conclusions was quite startling – especially when released thirty years after the event. In effect, it said that if the EEC was looking like a success, Britain might eventually have to join.[1]

The creation of the EEC saw the development of the institutions set up under the ECSC. Thus, the assembly and the court of justice for the ECSC became those for all three bodies, while the High Authority evolved into the Commission.

Included in the Treaty of Rome was the development of the Common Agricultural Policy (CAP). The CAP did not get off the ground until January 1962, however. While the CAP is examined in chapter 4, it is important to note here that its primary aim was to make the EEC self-sufficient in food production. There was to be no chance of the EEC member states ever being dependent upon food imports. Thus, vast sums of money were pumped into the agricultural sector to improve levels of food production.

This early development of the EEC is often seen as the heyday of co-operation between the six member states. Yet this is the picture seen through rose-tinted spectacles. It was not quite as straightforward as it is presented in some history books. An obvious example of the fraught relationship can be seen in 1965–66, which led to the **Luxembourg Compromise**.

In 1965, there was a dispute over how the CAP should be funded. It had been suggested that the power be taken away from the Council of Ministers and handed to the Commission and the Assembly. The French president, Charles de Gaulle, refused to accept such a move. A meeting was set to resolve the situation. The French were in the chair (as they held the presidency of the Council of Ministers). The meeting broke up very quickly with nothing resolved. The French government recalled its officials, leaving an 'empty-chair' presidency.

The situation was eventually resolved by what was called the 'Luxembourg Compromise'. In effect, this 'agreement to differ' gave each member state a veto over any decisions if it was of vital national interest. It was not termed quite so crudely but stated that the members had to work together to achieve unanimity in their decision-making. The dispute over the funding of the CAP was not revisited.

The first enlargement – Britain joins

After seeing the initial success of the EEC, the British government decided to organise an alternative to it. This was the European Free Trade Association (EFTA) which was set up in 1960. The idea behind EFTA was to promote free trade rather than to create some sort of supranational organisation. For the EFTA countries, the trade was to be in industrial goods – again a difference with the EEC which seemed, at this stage, to be focusing upon agricultural production. There were seven founder members of EFTA – Austria, Denmark, Finland, Norway, Portugal, Sweden and Britain. EFTA was not overly successful, however, especially from a British perspective. The benefits for Britain were marginal when trading with the other EFTA states whose economies were far smaller than that of Britain. Consequently, Britain and other EFTA members applied to join the EEC.

Britain first applied to join the EEC in 1961 under Harold Macmillan's Conservative Government, its application led by the Chief Negotiator Edward Heath. This application was vetoed by President de Gaulle. He feared that, by letting Britain join the EEC, it would be the 'Trojan horse' that would let the United States interfere in European matters. In his opinion, Britain was rather subservient to American whims. In 1956, Britain had backed out of the Suez venture, when Israel, Britain and France had colluded to invade Egypt to re-internationalise the Suez Canal. Britain had backed down as a result of US pressure. When Britain's independent nuclear deterrent project, Blue Streak, was scrapped, it was to the United States that Britain turned rather than to Europe. It must be noted that, while de Gaulle was opposed to British membership, the same could not be said of the other EEC members. They were more enthusiastic, but there was a requirement for unanimous decision-making. Added to this, there was a feeling among some EEC officials that, with her commitments to the United States (via the 'special relationship') and to the Commonwealth, Britain was not quite ready to join the EEC. Thus, this first application was vetoed in 1963.

A second application was made in 1967 – this time by the Labour Government of Harold Wilson. Again, this application was vetoed by de Gaulle. Britain had been forced to devalue the pound in mid-1967, and de Gaulle claimed that he could not let such a weak currency enter the EEC and drag down the collective European economy. Added to this, de Gaulle felt that Britain was still too 'Atlanticist' rather than being 'European'. Despite being under great strain, and made worse by Britain's refusal to send troops to Vietnam, the 'special relationship' with the United States was still seen as being paramount to Britain. It made it easy for de Gaulle to veto Britain's second application. Again, as with the first application, only the French government seemed to oppose British membership.

A third application was made in 1971. De Gaulle was no longer President of France, so one potential obstacle had gone. His successor, Georges Pompidou, was far more enthusiastic about **enlargement** to include Britain. These were also the first negotiations where a collective EEC position was developed. In all previous applications, the applicant states had to negotiate with all six member states separately.

In the 1970 General Election both major political parties in Britain had committed themselves to negotiating terms of entry – although neither committed itself to joining. Thus, arguably, Prime Minister Edward Heath did not have a mandate to take Britain into the EEC. This position was highlighted with all of the other applicant countries holding national referendums on membership. In their respective referendums Denmark and Ireland registered strong support for membership but the Norwegians voted against by a margin of 54 to 46 per cent. On 1 January 1973, however, after some tortuous negotiations[2] and referendums, Britain, Denmark and Ireland joined the EEC.

Yet the tale of Britain's application does not end here. In the February 1974 General Election, the Labour Party committed itself to renegotiating the terms of entry and then putting these new terms to a national referendum. Harold Wilson argued that the Heath Government had not got the best possible deal for Britain or for the Commonwealth. Added to this, there had never been a mandate to enter the EEC, and the public needed to be consulted. Thus, upon gaining office, Wilson ordered that the terms of entry be renegotiated. Once done, these would be put to a referendum – which was held in June 1975.

Arguably, the referendum had little to do with the EEC, and everything to do with keeping the Labour Party in office. Both major parties were divided on whether or not to remain in the EEC. Therefore, the party whip was suspended for the referendum. It was agreed that, once the people had decided this issue, it would be put to rest. With the party whip suspended, there were some curious bed fellows on each side of the referendum debate. On the 'No' side were Enoch Powell and Tony Benn. Powell was well to the right of the Conservative Party, while Benn was definitely on the left of the Labour Party. In the 'Yes' camp, there were key members of the Conservative, Labour and Liberal parties. This strong central base won through. The 'No' camp was presented as the extremes of British politics, including Marxists and fascists, as well as some prominent British politicians, as mentioned earlier. The 'Yes' camp was portrayed as representing the centre ground of British politics, that is, mainstream, common-sense politics. On a turnout of 63 per cent, two-thirds of voters supported continued membership of the EEC.

Enlargement to the south

The first enlargement comprised northern European countries. The next two enlargements (Greece in 1981 and Portugal and Spain in 1986) have been described as the southern or Mediterranean enlargements. All three states had been under the control of military juntas for many years. In the 1970s, democratic elections were held. A key step in strengthening these fledgling democracies was seen to be Community membership. The economies of all three countries were strongly agrarian, although parts of northern Spain were quite industrialised. This was to put some strain on the CAP. There was also a number of issues, particularly with Spanish membership, over fishing rights. All three economies were also quite weak – well below the Community average. There was strong pressure to grant development funds to all three states, but this was to be phased in. To have done otherwise would have damaged many regions of the nine member states which were dependent upon regional-development funding. There were also concerns about economic migrants – people leaving these poorer countries in search of jobs in the wealthier member states. The overarching aim of getting Spain and Portugal more integrated into Western Europe prevailed, however.

The European Union

The European Community was not just getting larger, it was also gradually becoming more integrated. There were stepping stones towards the creation of the **European Union** – most notably the Single European Act (SEA), the creation of the Single Market, and the Treaty of European Union (TEU) which was signed at Maastricht. The whole issue of integration versus expansion is examined in greater detail in chapter 7. The steps towards the formation of the European Union are noted here, however.

The Single European Act was the launch pad for the Single Market – the idea of no internal frontiers within the European Community. This was a small step in the integration of the Community members, and it quickly became clear that further steps needed to be taken. The SEA became law in 1987 and the Single Market came into effect in 1993. The idea of the Single Market was based upon what were described as the 'four freedoms': freedom of movement for goods, people, capital and services. States could no longer interfere in cross-border transactions between member states.

There was also a political aspect to the SEA. Most notably, while it did not challenge the Luxembourg Compromise, it did extend qualified majority voting to the Single Market programme. The SEA also increased the importance of the European Parliament. Although some member states were resistant to this move, increased consultation between the Council of Ministers and the European Parliament was introduced – known as the 'co-operation procedure' This is examined in greater detail in chapter 3.

Looked at in retrospect, the SEA was a springboard towards the formation of the European Union and the introduction of the single currency. Had this been so obvious at the time, it is highly unlikely that the British government, led by Margaret Thatcher, would have forced the legislation through the House of Commons on a guillotined debate and a three-line whip. Thatcher saw the SEA as an economic agreement, and seemingly ignored the politics.

The Treaty of European Union (TEU, but also known as the Maastricht Treaty) extended the economic developments of the SEA but also gave added powers to the European institutions. The European Parliament, for example, had its powers extended from 'co-operation' to 'co-decision maker'. Other areas of structural development included the creation of a European Ombudsman and the formation of the Committee of Regions.

As well as structural developments to the European Union, there were also policy changes. Included in the TEU was the plan to develop a single currency for the organisation. At this time, it was only a proposal. There were no steps outlined, nor a timetable proposed. There were other policy developments, including the Social Charter (to which Britain negotiated an opt-out), public health policy and transport.

This move towards a European Union saw the development of the idea of the three pillars. The first 'pillar' was the organisation that already existed – the European Community, with the single market, common policies, the structural funds, etc. The second 'pillar' of the EU was the Common Foreign and Security Policy (CFSP). This policy is examined in chapter 4. Briefly, it covers how the EU tries to influence foreign affairs – in some respects it is to do with the development of the identity of the EU at the international level.

The third 'pillar' of the EU is Justice and Home Affairs. If the CFSP is to do with external security, the Justice and Home Affairs pillar is about internal security. As with the CFSP, this third pillar tries to establish common positions rather than a common policy. Subject areas include asylum, drugs, police co-operation, etc. Both the second and the third pillars of the EU are very much intergovernmental – the different governments of the member states working together (see chapter 6). Collectively, the EC, the CFSP and Justice and Home Affairs combine as the three pillars of the European Union.

Throughout the negotiations for the TEU, Britain appeared to adopt a far more positive approach. Prime Minister John Major went into the negotiations with a wish list, as well as with a list of things to which his government objected. The results were such that Major was praised for his negotiating skills by pro- and anti-TEU campaigners alike. Having said this, Major had severe difficulties in getting the TEU ratified by Parliament. There was no referendum, unlike in Denmark where the TEU was initially rejected before a second referendum ratified the treaty.

Subsequent to the TEU, there have been two other treaties – Amsterdam and Nice. The Amsterdam Treaty (1997) developed the TEU further. This was carried out after the northern enlargement (see below). There had been plans for the Amsterdam Treaty to develop a proper political union, in line with what had been developed in the economic sphere by the SEA and the TEU. Yet these plans were never realised. There were some changes to areas such as asylum-seekers, immigration, social policy and the environment. Added to this, Britain repealed its opt-out from the Social Charter. There were also attempts to make the European Union more transparent in its operations.

The Treaty of Nice (2001) prepared the European Union for further enlargement – to the east. There were very complicated negotiations, which included a complete overhaul of the structures of the EU. This was needed to cope with a proposed enlargement of twelve member states, with others also queuing to join. The structures and processes of the European Union could not cope with a potential membership of as many as twenty-seven or thirty countries. As with the Amsterdam Treaty, the Treaty of Nice failed to live up to expectations. There was much tinkering done to the institutions (as will be seen in chapter 3) but the larger countries were unwilling to surrender their dominant position within the EU. The whole process was also complicated by the Republic of Ireland. According to the Irish constitution, the Treaty of Nice had to be subjected to a referendum. The Irish, like the Danes in 1992, voted against the treaty. Instructions issued from the Commission were that the Irish had to hold a second referendum and to get the right result! This was duly done.

The one prominent success story in the development of the European Union was the successful introduction of the single currency – the euro – in 2002. The criteria for joining had been laid down in the TEU although no timetable had been laid out. The convergence criteria – to harmonise all currencies that were to be replaced by the euro – appeared quite stringent. There were limits on national budget deficits, as well as on public debt. There were also constraints upon interest rates. Britain, Denmark and Sweden opted out of the single currency. Of the twelve states which eventually joined the euro, all had allegations made against them that they had fudged the convergence criterion. Regardless, the single currency went ahead.

The northern enlargement

After the success of creating the European Union, there came the opportunity for further enlargement. This must be seen in conjunction with the fall of the Berlin Wall, the demise of Soviet domination of Eastern Europe and the reunification of Germany. German reunification took place in 1990, prior to the creation of the EU. Through reunification, East Germany was able to join the then European Community without even applying or meeting any of the criteria for joining. As a result, not only did many East European countries request membership – especially in the light of the treatment of East Germany – but also countries that had remained neutral throughout the **Cold War** period. Four countries' applications were considered – Austria, Finland, Sweden and Norway. As in 1973, the Norwegians were accepted into the Union but then held a referendum whereby the people voted against membership. Thus in 1995, the twelve became fifteen.

This enlargement has been considered to have been the easiest of all. The three countries were economically advanced, were not dependent upon the CAP, and would become net contributors to the EU budget. As members of the European Free Trade Association, they had already taken steps to align their economies with that of the EU. EFTA members have associate membership of the EU. Added to this, they had also taken on board much of the EU legislation which applied in all member states (known as the *acquis communautaire*).

The European Union grows to the east

The most recent enlargement has been to include countries formerly under Soviet domination, together with Malta and Cyprus. (A summary of all enlargements is presented in Table 2.1.) Whereas the 1995 enlargement was fairly straightforward, the 2004 version was anything but. Originally, there were ten East European applicants, along with the two Mediterranean island states. The Bulgarian and Romanian applications were put on hold, however, as neither country was considered to have a sufficiently developed economy to join. They failed the **Copenhagen Criteria**.

The Copenhagen Criteria had been applied in the previous enlargement process. As the countries had sufficiently developed economies, this posed little problem. For the countries of Eastern Europe, it was far more complicated. Having introduced a market economy after Soviet withdrawal, all East European economies were fragile. This was exacerbated by the political circumstances in these fledgling democracies. In fact, the political situation was remarkably similar to those of Greece, Spain and Portugal in the late 1970s and early 1980s. As at that time, there were fears in many of the fifteen member states that economic migrants would flee Eastern Europe in search of jobs in the wealthier West. Parts of the British media were predicting millions of East Europeans entering Britain within months of joining the European Union.

There are three strands to the Copenhagen Criteria. The first focuses on the political institutions. Here the emphasis is upon democratic rights for all citizens, the importance of the rule of law, and

Table 2.1 Summary of the enlargements of the European Economic Community/European Union

1 January 1973	Denmark, Ireland, United Kingdom
1 January 1981	Greece
1 January 1986	Portugal, Spain
1 January 1995	Austria, Finland, Sweden
1 May 2004	Cyprus, Czech Republic, Estonia, Hungary, Latvia, Lithuania, Malta, Poland, Slovakia, Slovenia

protection of minority rights. The second strand is economic. There is a need for a functioning market economy. This economy must be able to cope with the rigours and demands set on it through complying with all EU law. Finally, there are the obligations of membership – this is the third strand. Here the emphasis is upon adhering to the aims of political, economic and monetary union.

The 2004 enlargement was the most problematic of all. The eight East European countries were underdeveloped economically, especially when compared with the rest of the European Union. The enlargement was so big that all the EU institutions needed to be re-evaluated. Thus there were huge changes to all the EU institutions. For example, the number of MEPs from each member state was reassessed, as was the number of commissioners. All this is examined in greater detail in chapter 3.

As with the enlargements to the south (Greece, Spain and Portugal), EU monies from such things as the CAP were to be phased in gradually over a period of ten years. Most of the newcomers argued that they had the right to receive the full amount from the budget upon gaining membership. In this, they were to be disappointed. Full funding had been phased in during the Mediterranean enlargement – thus, a precedent had been set. The new member states had to continue to modernise their economies from within. There would be only some EU money to help. A consequence of this has been an upsurge in feeling against EU membership in most of the new member states.

Who is the 'reluctant European'?

This is an important aspect of this book, and one which will be returned to repeatedly. The final chapter will address the question in full but a number of important points needs to be noted.

First of all, there is the question of 'what is a **reluctant European**?' The answer to this question will then determine who are labelled the reluctant Europeans. For example, if a 'reluctant European' is a country which does not want to be a member of the European Union, then there is a number of candidate countries. Top of the list would be Norway, which has applied twice, been accepted twice, but then rejected the offer in national referendums twice. Another country which does not seem to want to take part in the European experiment is Switzerland. Finally, there is Greenland. As part of Denmark, Greenland gained EEC membership in 1973. Greenland withdrew in 1982, however.

It could be argued that, during the early years of the ECSC and the EEC, Britain was a 'reluctant European' – using the same criteria that have been applied to Norway and others. In the 1950s Britain chose not to join. That this position was reversed in the 1960s would clearly show that, if being a 'reluctant European' meant not being involved with the organisation at all, then by 1961, Britain was no longer a 'reluctant European'.

At the other end of the scale is the idea that a 'reluctant European' is a country that does not participate in the European experiment with any degree of enthusiasm. There is participation – that is, membership – but there seems to be a dragging of feet at times. While this is still a rather vague description of a 'reluctant European', it highlights a problem. Almost every member state could be described as a 'reluctant European' at some time or another. The French could gain the label through forcing the Luxembourg Compromise, the Danes for not ratifying the TEU at the first attempt, the Irish over the Nice Treaty and for not supporting the East European enlargement, the Swedes for voting against joining the euro; all those members that are unenthusiastic about further enlargement (or even previous enlargements), or even those who are unenthused about reforming the CAP, could be described as 'reluctant European'.

Yet the country that has received the label 'reluctant European' is Britain. There is a long list of reasons why such a label has been used. At first, there was reluctance to join. Upon joining, the terms of entry were renegotiated. There was a demand from one particular prime minister for 'our money back', and she repeated this demand frequently before getting a special budgetary rebate, which has since been guarded zealously. There were frequent refusals throughout the 1980s to join in the European Monetary System. During the negotiations on the TEU, John Major refused to allow the word 'federal' to be used in the treaty – although he was willing to allow 'ever closer union', which is a phrase with far stronger connotations of a single superstate. More recently, Britain has refused to join the euro. Specific barriers, notably Gordon Brown's 'Five Economic Tests', have made it increasingly difficult for Britain to join. On top of all of this, as feared by de Gaulle, Britain continually looks to the United States rather than to Europe. The war in Iraq is a clear example.

The above list seems quite comprehensive. Britain is a 'reluctant European'. Yet, at times, Britain is also proactive in its membership of the European Union. For example, Britain has been to the forefront in combating fraud in the EU. Britain has been one of the strongest advocates for reform of the CAP. During the negotiations on the TEU, it was the British government that was able to develop a European Ombudsman. Currently, Britain is eager to develop a European Rapid Reaction Force to work alongside NATO. This would enhance the EU's role as a 'regional police force'. All of this would suggest that Britain is not as reluctant a European as is sometimes portrayed.

So who is the 'reluctant European'? The answer is not obvious. It could apply to almost any member state. Britain earns the label as it is one of the largest countries in the European Union, and one of the most vocal when it comes to opposing some schemes that have been proposed by the EU. Yet, once decisions are made, Britain is consistent in enforcing the EU decisions. The label is harsh. Arguably, it was justified prior to EEC membership and even during the Thatcher years. Since then, it is not nearly so clear-cut. It just seems to be that other members' foibles are not so widely and loudly pointed out.

....

✔ What you should have learnt from reading this chapter

- The European Union of today has developed from the European Coal and Steel Community of the early 1950s. The founding father was Jean Monnet. The process of moving from ECSC to the EU has been gradual.

- There have been several stages of enlargement. The first, in 1973, included Britain. The most recent included eight East European countries which had previously been under Soviet domination, as well as the island states of Malta and Cyprus.

- The concept 'reluctant European' is one that has been given to Britain. There is a number of problems here, however. The first is the difficulty in explaining the concept. Different interpretations mean that different countries may be worthy of the label. The second is that, while Britain appears to be reluctant at times, so do many other member states.

🔎 Glossary of key terms

Acquis communautaire This is all the EU legislation that must be taken on board by any state joining the organisation. It includes policies as well as legislation.

Cold War The period of dispute between the United States and the Soviet Union after World War II. It is described as a 'cold' war as there was no actual fighting between the protagonists. At times, there was fighting between proxies. The war itself was ideological – capitalism versus communism – and was over hearts and minds, rather than actual fighting. When there is fighting, it would be a 'hot' war.

Copenhagen Criteria These are the criteria that any member state must meet to be able to join the European Union. They look at political institutions (democracy), the economy (it must be market dominated), and an applicant state must also be able to cope with the rigours of membership.

Enlargement This is where the European Union increases the number of its members. There have been several enlargements – 1973, 1981, 1986, 1995 and 2004.

Euratom The European Atomic Agency was set up alongside the EEC. Its aim was to focus on developing a nuclear energy programme for economic purposes.

European Coal and Steel Community (ECSC) The original founding body of the EU. It was created by the Schuman Plan which led to the Treaty of Paris. The ECSC came into being in 1952 with a life expectancy of fifty years.

European Defence Community (EDC) A European defence pact that was drawn up in 1952 to include West Germany in the defence of Western Europe against possible Soviet invasion. It was never ratified.

European Economic Community (EEC) The Treaty of Rome is the founding document of this organisation. It was set up in 1957 to integrate further the economies of the ECSC members beyond simply coal and steel.

European Free Trade Association (EFTA) A body set up to counteract the EEC. The emphasis was upon free trade, particularly in industrial goods. There was to be no surrender of sovereignty.

European Union (EU) The EU was established via the Treaty of European Union (TEU), signed at Maastricht in 1991. It extended the economic integration of the member states, as well as the political integration. More powers were given to the EU institutions, especially the European Parliament.

Luxembourg Compromise All member states have a veto over policy proposals if they constitute a serious threat to national interests.

Monnet, Jean The founding father of the ECSC. Monnet was the brains behind integrating aspects of the French and West German economies to prevent further wars between the two countries. He became the first president of the ECSC High Authority.

Reluctant European This label is usually applied to Britain. It suggests that Britain is not overly enthusiastic about EU membership. There is a number of different interpretations of the term, however, ranging from not wishing to join the EU to being a problematic member. If the former label is used, then Britain is no longer a 'reluctant European'. If the latter label is used, almost every member of the EU could be described as reluctant.

Sovereignty The right of a state to pass laws within its own territory. It is suggested that EU membership undermines national sovereignty as all members have to cede a range of powers to the EU. Added to this, EU law overrides national law when the two conflict.

Special relationship This term is used to describe the close relationship between the United States and Britain. Their close relationship, enhanced through ties of language, has been highlighted by successive British governments as the key underpinning of British foreign policy. This has led to accusations that Britain looks to the United States rather than to the EU. Some British governments have perceived their role as a bridge between the US and Europe.

Supranationalism When powers are ceded to the EU institutions, it suggests a movement towards supranationalism. This is especially the case when the EU is able to force member states to adopt particular policies, even if there is national reluctance.

? Likely examination questions

Why did Britain earn the label 'reluctant European'? To what extent is it still justified?

'The enlargement process has gone too far. The European Union is now too big and too unwieldy. There should be no further enlargements.' Discuss.

Why are the Single European Act (SEA) and the Treaty of European Union (TEU) perceived as stepping stones towards creating a federal Europe?

Helpful websites

The EU has a calendar of key events at europa.eu.int/abc/history/index_ en.htm. The coverage is a comprehensive timeline, but with no analysis.

For a brief potted history of the development of the EU, going back to 1919, a very useful site is www.historiasiglo20.org/europe. Although this is a Spanish site, this particular section is in English.

Suggestions for further reading

S. Burgess and G. Edwards, 'The Six Plus One: British Policy-making and the Question of European Economic Integration, 1955', *International Affairs*, vol. 64 no. 3 (1988) pp. 393–413.

M. Camps, *Britain and the European Community, 1955–1963* (Oxford University Press, 1964).

S. George, *Britain and European Integration since 1945* (Basil Blackwell, 1991).

U. Kitzinger, *Diplomacy and Persuasion: how Britain Joined the Common Market* (Thames and Hudson, 1973).

U. Kitzinger and D. Butler, *The 1975 Referendum* (Macmillan, 1976).

S. Young, *Terms of Entry: Britain's Negotiations with the European Community 1970–1972* (Heinemann, 1973).

CHAPTER 3

Institutions of the European Union

Contents

Overview

The institutions of the European Union have evolved as the organisation has developed. Each of them has acquired new powers although there has also been some movement towards sharing power. The whole idea of sharing power between the institutions of the EU has not always been greeted enthusiastically. Added to this, the member states are often reluctant to cede powers to the EU institutions. Where new bodies have been created, the older, more established bodies have been reluctant to share power with them. This has caused some problems for the EU as a whole. This chapter will examine how the different institutions have evolved from those set up in the 1950s. There will be a greater focus on the current powers of the major EU institutions. There will also be an analysis of some of the newer institutions, however – including those created by the Treaty of European Union.

Key issues to be covered in this chapter

- The major institutions of the European Union – Commission, Council of Ministers, COREPER, European Council, Parliament and the Court of Justice
- How these bodies have developed
- The powers of these different bodies
- The newer bodies – Committee of Regions, Ombudsman and the Economic and Social Committee
- Britain's role within all the EU institutions
- The 'democratic deficit'

The Commission

The **European Commission** receives much bad press in Britain. It is often portrayed as a giant octopus, attempting to get its tentacles into every aspect of British lives. Thus we hear stories of the Commission issuing regulations that will ban the British sausage, or compel donkey owners working on beaches to put nappies on their donkeys to keep the beaches clean. The problem is that there may be a grain of truth in the proposals, but not in the way in which many of these stories are reported.

What makes the situation even worse is that the Commission is anything but transparent. It is very difficult to find out what the Commission actually does. On top of this, the Commission is appointed. It then appears to be very difficult to hold the commissioners to account for their actions. Perhaps it is no wonder that the Commission receives such bad press.

The Commission was set up under the Treaty of Rome which established the European Economic Community. Arguably, its predecessor was the High Authority of the European Coal and Steel Community (ECSC). With the merger of the ECSC, EEC and Euratom in 1967, the High Authority and the Commission were merged into a single body.

The Commission is involved in the decision-making processes of the European Union at all levels. While it is often presented as being the civil service of the EU, its role is actually far more complicated. The Commission does draw up legislative proposals but these are for the consideration of the other EU institutions. Once the laws are 'passed', the Commission is then involved in their implementation – although this is often done at the national level rather than at the EU level.

As well as being involved in the law-making processes of the European Union, the Commission is also known as the 'Guardian of the Treaties'. This means that the Commission attempts to make sure that all member states uphold the various treaties of the EU – the letter as well as the spirit of the treaties. The Commission also works towards developing 'ever-close union' within the EU.

A major problem for the Commission is that it stands at the crossroads between intergovernmentalism and supranationalism. This debate is examined in chapter 6 but a brief point needs to be made

---

Box 3.1: The laws of the European Union

Many different laws are passed by the European Union. They are often portrayed as being some sort of blanket legislation covering the entire EU but this is not always the case. The EU can make legislation in a number of areas, and these are growing. There is a number of different types of legislation:

- *Regulations*

These are the most powerful of the EU laws. They are binding in every respect on all member states. This means that the EU is not only telling all member states what to do, but also how to do it.

- *Directives*

These are binding on the member states. How they are implemented is left up to the national governments. Thus the aim or objective of the legislation is made clear but the way in which this is achieved is left up to the national government's discretion.

- *Decisions*

These are binding on the member states, organisations or individuals to which they are addressed.

- *Recommendations and Opinions*

These are purely advisory. They are not binding in any way. Recommendations and opinions are often used to 'test the water' on some new EU proposals.

---

here. The supranational aspect of the Commission (which tends to dominate) sees the Commission as working towards greater integration and ultimately to a proper European union. The Commissioners are all supposed to work towards this goal. Yet there is also an intergovernmental aspect as well. Each member state gets to nominate its 'national' commissioner – every member state has its own commissioner. Each commissioner is supposed to work for the Commission rather than for his or her national government but the national nomination has some impact.

Currently, there are twenty-five commissioners. With each future enlargement, the number of commissioners is likely to grow unless there is some fundamental reform of the Commission that breaks away from the national nomination. The Commission is headed by a president. This post is currently held by José Manuel Barroso. His Commission is listed in Table 3.1

Each commissioner is allocated a portfolio by the president. National governments may nominate their members but they have limited input into the allocation of portfolios. At best, they can lobby the president for specific posts but there is no compunction for the president to listen. In 2004, there was a huge outcry from the French that 'their' commissioner was given the rather unimportant post of Transport. The position of joint vice-president did not soothe the ire of the French. There was nothing that the French government could do, however.

The only body that can block the appointment of commissioners is the European Parliament – and such a block happened in 2004. Barroso presented his nominations to the European Parliament. The Parliament can either accept or reject the proposed Commission. Many MEPs took exception to the Italian nominee (Rocco Buttiglione) and his specified portfolio. He was opposed to gay rights and to some aspects of women's rights, and was being proposed to the post of Justice, Freedom and Security. Neither Barroso nor the Italian government would retract the nomination, so the European Parliament rejected the entire Commission. Buttiglione stood down and the Italian government presented an alternative nomination. A few other changes were made and the European Parliament accepted the proposed Commission.

At the time of writing, Britain's commissioner is Peter Mandelson. He has been allocated one of the key portfolios – Trade. This means that Mandelson, as the EU's representative, is able to negotiate trade treaties with the United States, China, Japan and other states around the world. While the Trade portfolio is a powerful one, it is also a very tricky one. It is very easy to upset member states as a result of negotiating tactics, or to create an impasse with other countries over trade-related issues. For example, in 2005, Mandelson had to resolve the trade dispute between the European Union and China, as the Chinese had exceeded their export quotas to the EU.

The Commission has a number of roles to play and a variety of powers. The first of these, which has already been noted, is the power to propose and develop legislation. Arguably, this is the most important

Table 3.1   The Barroso Commission (appointed November 2004)

Name	Country	Portfolio
José Manuel Barroso	**Portugal**	**President**
Margot Wallström	Sweden	Institutional Relations and Communications Strategy (Vice-President)
Günter Verheugen	Germany	Entreprise and Industry (Vice-President)
Jacques Barrot	France	Transport (Vice-President)
Siim Kallas	Estonia	Administrative Affairs, Audit and Anti-fraud (Vice-President)
Franco Frattini	Italy	Justice, Freedom and Security (Vice-President)
Viviane Reding	Luxembourg	Information Society and Media
Stavros Dimas	Greece	Environment
Joaquín Almunia	Spain	Economic and Monetary Affairs
Danuta Hübner	Poland	Regional Policy
Joe Borg	Malta	Fisheries and Maritime Affairs
Dalia Grybauskaitė	Lithuania	Financial Programming and Budget
Janez Potočnik	Slovenia	Science and Research
Ján Figeľ	Slovakia	Education, Training, Culture and Multilingualism
Markos Kyprianou	Cyprus	Health and Consumer Protection
Olli Rehn	Finland	Enlargement

Table 3.1 (continued)		
Name	**Country**	**Portfolio**
Louis Michel	Belgium	Development and Humanitarian Aid
László Kovács	Hungary	Taxation and Customs Union
Neelie Kroes-Smit	Netherlands	Competition
Marian Fischer Boel	Denmark	Agriculture and Rural Development
Benita Ferrero-Waldner	Austria	External Relations and European Neighbourhood Policy
Charlie McCreevy	Ireland	Internal Market and Services
Vladimir Špidia	Czech Republic	Employment, Social Affairs and Equal Opportunities
Peter Mandelson	UK	Trade
Andris Piebalgs	Latvia	Energy

role played by the Commission. The power to propose legislation lies with the Commission alone – although any proposals must be accepted by the European Parliament and the Council of Ministers.

A second power is responsibility for the EU budget. Not only does the Commission draft the budget and guide it through the Council of Ministers and the European Parliament, but it also administers the spending by the EU. The Commission makes sure that revenue is collected and that accounts are accurate where there is spending.

The Commission is also the external representative of the EU. Like any country, the EU has established embassies (or, more accurately, offices) around the world. The Commission deals with the United Nations and with other international organisations, including the G8.

There is a prominent role for the Commission as the 'Guardian of the Treaties'. In effect, this means that the Commission has to make sure that all member states are upholding both the spirit and the letter of the various treaties that have been drawn up; for example, the Treaty of Rome, the Treaty of European Union, as well as other legislation that has been ratified by the EU.

Finally, the Commission is also the conscience of the EU. This can be seen as the role of mediator between conflicting interests, be they between member states or member states and other EU institutions. The whole idea of the Commission is to promote the general interests of the EU. It has to act above simple national interests and perform a supranational role.

The European Council

The **European Council** is sometimes perceived to be little more than an extension of the Council of Ministers. It could also be seen as the upper tier of the **Council of Ministers**. In this respect, the European Council is far more powerful than the Council of Ministers. It can set the agenda for the Council of Ministers and for the Commission, and can override or even ignore the **European Parliament** as well. Technically, however, the European Council is not part of the Council of Ministers. It merely has the power and authority to override the Council of Ministers.

The European Council began to meet in 1974. It was not until the Single European Act, however, that these meetings or summits were given formal recognition. These summits are held twice a year, and are chaired by the country holding the presidency of the Council of Ministers. The summits last for only two days but are very intensive. In the past they have been held in regional cities of the host state but now they tend to be held in Brussels. All heads of government attend, along with their foreign ministers. The President of the Commission and the vice-presidents also attend. Added to this, there are numerous other informal meetings. Some of these may relate to specific issues. When Britain held the presidency of the European Council, an informal meeting of all heads of state was held in October 2005 at Hampton Court Palace in Surrey. There was also the formal summit in Brussels in December 2005.

Every summit is a high-profile event, but it has led to accusations that European Council meetings have become little more than public-relations exercises where all the member states get together and mouth platitudes of agreement on a number of issues, knowing full well that nothing will actually be done. The reality is somewhat different.

The European Council sets the strategic policy direction for the European Union. In a number of areas, the European Council is able to make key decisions. These areas include political and economic integration, foreign policy, budgetary disputes, and on new applicants. Thus, the origins of the Treaty of Nice (2000) – which enabled the 2004 enlargement to go ahead – were in a European Council summit.

The European Council performs in an intergovernmental and in a supranational fashion. It is an intergovernmental body, in that national interests are defended, but it is also supranational in that, when the decisions are taken, they affect all members, as well as potential future members, of the European Union. The European Council is able to influence all aspects of the EU.

The Council of Ministers

This body is also known as the **Council of the European Union** or, simply, the Council. Such terminology often confuses people, especially when the European Council is included in discussions. Therefore, for the sake of simplicity, the term Council of Ministers will be used in this book.

The Council of Ministers is the dominant body of the European Union. It is still the major decision-making body of the EU although, since the Treaty of European Union, it has been forced to cede some powers and influence to the European Parliament. They are now co-decision-makers. The Council of Ministers is assisted by a body known as COREPER (Committee of Permanent Representatives). The role and function of COREPER are examined in the next section of this chapter.

Although the label 'Council of Ministers' is used, arguably there are several councils. For example, when agriculture is under discussion, each member state's agriculture minister will be in attendance.

If it is energy, then the energy ministers will attend. When finances are under discussion, it will be the finance ministers who attend. Thus, when there are council meetings, it is not necessarily going to be the same personnel in attendance on each occasion.

To complicate matters a little further, there is a rotating presidency. This had already been noted in the section on the European Council. Each country takes a turn for a six-month period. During this time, the 'president' can set the agenda for the Council of Ministers. When Britain held the presidency in the second half of 2005, the issue of Turkish negotiations for EU membership had to be resolved. Britain was very keen for Turkey to join the EU but other member states, most notably Austria, were less enthusiastic. The future rotations of the presidency are listed in Table 3.2. Note where Bulgaria and Romania (who are expected to join the EU in 2007) first hold the presidency.

The rotation is very important. A country holding the presidency in the first half of the year is involved in preparing the budget. Thus, each member state will hold the presidency in alternating halves of the year. For example, Britain held the presidency in the first half of 1998 and the second half of 2005. Assuming the rotating presidency continues, the United Kingdom will next hold the presidency in the second half of 2017, and its subsequent presidency after that will be in the first half of the year.

Decision-making in the Council of Ministers can be quite complicated. Each country has a number of votes, linked to its population size. This is presented in Table 3.3. Decisions are taken either through simple majorities, qualified majorities, or unanimity. Minor decisions are taken using simple majority voting, for example, on anti-dumping legislation. Issues such as enlargement are taken through unanimity – hence the difficulties that the Turks have continued to face in their application. Many decisions are taken by **qualified majority voting (QMV)**. To get any decisions made through QMV requires 232 out of the 321 votes. Alternatively, to block any proposals requires ninety votes. This means that three of the largest countries are not able to block any proposals. The United Kingdom, Germany and France would need the support of at least one other country to block a proposal that they did not like.

Though not directly elected, the Council of Ministers is the legislative part of the European Union. Since the Treaty of European

Table 3.2 Planned rotation of the presidency of the Council of Ministers

Country	Date of presidency
Austria	January – June 2006
Finland	July – December 2006
Germany	January – June 2007
Portugal	July – December 2007
Slovenia	January – June 2008
France	July – December 2008
Czech Republic	January – June 2009
Sweden	July – December 2009
Spain	January – June 2010
Belgium	July – December 2010
Hungary	January – June 2011
Poland	July – December 2011
Denmark	January – June 2012
Cyprus	July – December 2012
Ireland	January – June 2013
Lithuania	July – December 2013
Greece	January – June 2014
Italy	July – December 2014
Latvia	January – June 2015
Luxembourg	July – December 2015

Table 3.2 (continued)	
Country	**Date of presidency**
Netherlands	January – June 2016
Slovakia	July – December 2016
Malta	January – June 2017
UK	July – December 2017
Estonia	January – June 2018
Bulgaria	July – December 2018
Austria	January – June 2019
Romania	July – December 2019

Union, however, it has had to share aspects of this with the European Parliament. They are now co-decision makers. The co-decision procedure will be examined in the section on the European Parliament.

The Council of Ministers is normally perceived to be a part of the intergovernmental aspect of the European Union. It is in this body that national concerns are raised and often protected. Commitments to ever-closer union may often be mouthed but, in many cases, it is often to be NOT at the national expense. The intergovernmental aspects may dominate but there is also a gradual movement towards a more supranational approach as well. With the Union now standing at a membership of twenty-five, and Romania and Bulgaria soon to join, as well as a number of other countries, it is becoming more and more difficult to protect national interests. Margaret Thatcher once complained that Britain had surrendered too much **sovereignty**. It is even more the case now than when Thatcher was speaking in the late 1980s that the only way to protect a country's sovereignty is to 'surrender' some of it. Except in cases of extreme national importance, where the veto can be used, the only way for a country to achieve its objectives is to work with other members. It has

Table 3.3 Weights of votes in the Council of Ministers (2005)

Country	Population (millions)	Votes
Germany	82	29
UK	60	29
France	59	29
Italy	58	29
Spain	39	27
Poland	39	27
Netherlands	16	13
Greece	11	12
Belgium	10	12
Portugal	10	12
Czech Republic	10	12
Hungary	10	12
Sweden	9	10
Austria	8	10
Denmark	5	7
Finland	5	7
Slovakia	5	7
Ireland	4	7
Lithuania	4	7
Latvia	2	4
Slovenia	2	4

Table 3.3 (continued)		
Country	Population (millions)	Votes
Estonia	1	4
Cyprus	0.7	4
Luxembourg	0.4	4
Malta	0.4	3
Total	451.5	321

taken successive British governments a very long time to realise that collaboration is far more effective than confrontation. With the 2004 enlargement, there are now more member states that are closer in line to Britain's way of thinking as to how the EU should be run politically and economically. The British government needs these allies in the Council of Ministers to be able to achieve its aims.

COREPER

COREPER, or the Committee of Permanent Representatives, is the body that assists the Council of Ministers. It comprises civil servants and diplomats who are there to assist their governments. They are the resident national representatives – for example, UKREP are the British representatives.

Much of COREPER's work is secret. The permanent representatives (who are the national ambassadors to the European Union) and their teams meet their counterparts on a regular basis – normally weekly. In general terms, these permanent representatives prepare for meetings. Thus, they do all the legwork before a meeting of the Council of Ministers. This in itself suggests that these representatives may actually be involved in behind-the-scenes decision-making although, officially, they have no such power.

Since 1962, with the huge increase in work for COREPER, the body has been divided into two. COREPER 1 comprises the deputy permanent representatives, while COREPER 2 comprises the permanent representatives. There is a rigid division of work. Once a particular subject area has been designated to COREPER 1, for example, COREPER 2 then has nothing to do with it. Areas designated to COREPER 1 include fisheries, education, consumer affairs and health. COREPER 2 covers areas such as the budget, justice and home affairs, the structural and cohesion funds, and accession.

COREPER appears to be the symbol of intergovernmentalism; each member state has these officials there to protect national interests in behind-the-scenes negotiations. Yet this very role is also a symbol of supranationalism, as COREPER may have made the decisions prior to the meeting of the Council of Ministers. They simply have to sell the end result to the politicians.

The European Parliament

The European Parliament (EP) is the only body within the European Union that is directly elected – and this has been the case only since 1979. Its origins lie in the old assembly of the ECSC. Until 1979, members were appointed from national assemblies and parliaments.

Originally, the EP was perceived as little more than a talking shop. The Members of the European Parliament (MEPs) could discuss whatever issues they liked but the other institutions were under no obligation to listen to this advice. The situation today is totally different, with the EP having been granted the power of co-decision in the Treaty of European Union. The co-decision procedure will be examined below.

Although the body is known as the European Parliament, it is unlike any national parliament. For most countries, the national parliament or assembly is the legislative body. The EP has never played such a role. Even today, as **co-decision maker**, it is still dependent upon the Council of Ministers and the Commission in generating and ratifying legislative proposals.

Just as with the number of votes each member state has in the Council of Ministers, the number of MEPs for each country is dependent upon population. The number of MEPs for each member state is listed in Table 3.4. Although Germany has the largest number of MEPs (99), in relation to population size, Germany is still under-represented when compared with Luxembourg or Malta.

Table 3.4 The number MEPs for each member state

Country	Number of MEPs
Germany	99
UK	78
France	78
Italy	78
Spain	54
Poland	54
Netherlands	27
Greece	24
Belgium	24
Portugal	24
Czech Republic	24
Hungary	24
Sweden	19
Austria	18
Denmark	14
Finland	14
Slovakia	14
Ireland	13
Lithuania	13
Latvia	9
Slovenia	7

Table 3.4 (continued)	
Country	Number of MEPs
Estonia	6
Cyprus	6
Luxembourg	6
Malta	5
Total	732

When elected, the MEPs do not sit in national groups. Rather, they sit in what are termed ideological transnational groupings. To put it more simply, they sit with like-minded MEPs. In Table 3.5, you can see the different ideological groupings, as well as the locations of the British MEPs within this. Two of the non-attached British MEPs who are listed in the table were both originally elected as UKIP MEPs (Robert Kilroy Silk and Ashley Mote). Although elected as a Conservative MEP, Roger Helmer has chosen to sit with the non-attached MEPs rather than with the European People's Party (EPP). This seems to be an ideological decision as the EPP is committed to greater political and economic integration. The Conservatives in this grouping are uneasy bedfellows. Helmer refused to toe the party line but remained a Conservative MEP. This gives the East Midlands two MEPs sitting as non-attached members – the other being Kilroy Silk. With regard to the Conservative Party position on EPP membership, David Cameron has voiced the idea of withdrawing from this grouping. There is a standing commitment to remain in the grouping until 2009, however.

The elections to the European Parliament are held on a fixed five year term. These elections are held in June – thus the next elections will be in June 2009. The European Parliament does not use a single electoral system for the elections. In fact, the elections are not even held on a single day. Some countries hold their elections on a

Table 3.5 Make-up of the European Parliament (October 2005)

Transnational Grouping	Number of MEPs	British MEPs within the group
European People's Party and European Democrats	267	26 Conservative 1 Ulster Unionist
European Group of Socialists	201	19 Labour
Alliance of Liberals and Democrats for Europe	89	12 Liberal Democrats
Greens and European Free Alliance	42	2 Greens 2 Scottish Nationalist 2 Plaid Cymru
European United Left and Nordic Green Left	41	1 Sinn Fein
Independence/Democracy	36	10 UK Independence
Union for the Europe of the Nations	27	–
Non-attached	29	1 Democratic Unionist 1 Conservative 2 Independent (formerly UKIP)

Thursday (for example, Britain) while others hold theirs on a Sunday (for example, France). Despite the polling day, no ballots are counted until all polling stations are closed. Thus, British votes, though cast on a Thursday, are not counted until the following Sunday.

All EU states use some form of proportional representation for their elections to the European Parliament. This is a recent event, however. Mainland Britain used simple plurality until 1999 when they changed to the d'Hondt (closed-) list system. The UK actually utilises two electoral systems, however. The ballot in Northern Ireland is conducted under the single transferable vote (STV) and always has been since direct elections started in 1979. Different countries use different electoral systems for the elections to the European Parliament. In the 1994 elections (when there were only twelve member states), eight different electoral systems were used across the European Union.

The powers of the European Parliament have grown over time. In the 1960s and 1970s, it was dismissed as little more than a talking shop where national MPs had another forum in which to raise their voices. It did actually have some supervisory powers which it could wield, however.

One of these powers was known as 'the power of the purse'. In effect, from the mid-1970s, the European Parliament was given a supervisory role over the Community budget. The Commission puts forward its budgetary proposals and these have to be accepted by the European Parliament. The Parliament can either accept or reject the proposals. A rejection would mean that the European Union would then work on a series of twelfths from the previous year's budget – one twelfth of that budget each month.

Another supervisory power of the European Parliament has been over the appointment of the Commission. The Parliament can either accept or reject proposed appointments to the Commission. As noted earlier in this chapter, the first Barroso Commission was rejected in 2004.

Though not a legislative (law-making) body, the European Parliament has also increased its role in the legislative process. It can, for example, suggest new policies, or even laws, to the Commission. Yet, within the actual process of making the law, over time the European Parliament has acquired powers. The Treaty of Rome gave the European Parliament the power of *consultation*. This meant that the Parliament could give an opinion on any laws being proposed. Its opinion was non-binding, however. This was enhanced in the Single European Act (1986) which developed the power to that of *co-operation*. This was akin to giving the European Parliament a 'second reading' of legislative proposals. Within this process, the Council of Ministers has to explain why any proposed amendments suggested in the first 'con-sultation' have been rejected. Again, there is no requirement that the European Parliament's opinions be incorporated into any legislation. The difference here is that the Council of Ministers had to be unani-mous in rejecting the opinion of the European Parliament.

The co-operation process was developed further in the Treaty of European Union where the European Parliament was given the power of *co-decision*. The co-decision procedure was like a 'third reading' of some legislative proposals. In effect, as the name suggests, the European Parliament has become an equal co-decision-maker with the Council of Ministers.

Finally, there is the power of *assent*. This means that, in certain areas, the European Parliament must not only be consulted but must also give its agreement for policies to proceed. These areas include enlargement and signing of international agreements. For the European Parliament to support these decisions, a simple majority of MEPs is required.

What has been interesting about the development of the European Parliament is that, as it has acquired new or extended powers, it has been loath to surrender any powers to any other bodies. Thus, with the development of the **Committee of Regions**, the European Parliament made sure that this new body (which is examined below) received only powers of consultation.

The Court of Justice

The **Court of Justice** is based in Luxembourg. Its role is to make sure that all member states uphold EU laws as well as the various treaties of the European Union. This is not just the letter of the law but also the spirit of the law. The Court of Justice is restricted in what it can investigate, however.

First of all, the Court of Justice cannot be proactive in what it investigates. Cases must be referred to the Court. These cases can be referred by other institutions within the EU, by member states, or even by private organisations or individuals.

Secondly, the Court of Justice is restricted in what it can investigate. Law-making in the European Union is divided into what are national competences and what are EU competences. Under the principle of **subsidiarity**, some decision-making is devolved to the most appropriate level. If it is devolved to national, regional or even to a local tier of government, then it is not covered by the Court of Justice.

The membership of the Court of Justice demonstrates the extent to which it is still an intergovernmental body, even though all

members are supposed to be independent of their national governments. Currently, there are twenty-five judges, one from each
member state. Unlike in the US Court of Justice, they are all non-
political appointments. Each judge is appointed for a renewable six-
year term although he/she can stand down at any time. The judges
are assisted by advocates-general. There are eight of these advocates-
general, although this number may be increased at the request of the
Court of Justice but only if the Council of Ministers agrees unani-
mously. It is their job to review cases that come to the Court of Justice,
and to deliver opinions prior to judges seeing the cases. In some
respects, the advocates-general function as a filter.

As the workload for the Court of Justice increased, some reforms
were introduced. In 1988, the **Court of First Instance** was established to assist the Court of Justice. Originally, the Court of First
Instance was attached to the Court of Justice but that is no longer the
case. The role of the Court of First Instance is to improve the judicial scrutiny of factual matters. Thus, the Court of First Instance
examines points of fact while the Court of Justice examines points
of law. As with the Court of Justice, the Court of First Instance
has twenty-five judges – one from each member state. There are no
advocates-general to assist the Court of First Instance, however.

The Committee of Regions

The Committee of Regions was created by the Treaty of European
Union and came into being in 1994. It is an indirectly elected body,
comprising delegates from all member states who have been
elected (or in some cases, appointed) to regional or local tiers of government. Currently there are 317 members, with each country
having membership corresponding to its population size. This is
detailed in Table 3.6. As can be seen in that table, the largest members
each has twenty-four representatives; the smallest (Malta) has five.

The British members of the Committee of Regions come
from local government across the United Kingdom, the Scottish
Parliament, the Welsh Assembly, the Northern Ireland Assembly, the
Greater London Assembly, and the regional development agencies in
England. There is a requirement that the representation of any
country includes delegates of different political persuasions. The

Table 3.6 Membership of the Committee of Regions

Country	Number of members
France, Germany, Italy, UK	24
Poland, Spain	21
Austria, Belgium, Czech Republic, Greece, Hungary, Netherlands, Portugal, Sweden	12
Denmark, Finland, Ireland, Lithuania, Slovakia	9
Estonia, Latvia, Slovenia	7
Cyprus, Luxembourg	6
Malta	5

members do not sit in national groups. As in the European Parliament, they sit in ideological groupings. Arguably, this is an attempt to develop the supranational characteristics of the Committee.

The Committee of Regions has to be consulted on any policy proposals relating to local or regional government. This is to make sure that the idea of subsidiarity works effectively. While the body is purely advisory, it still has to be consulted on a number of areas. These include:

cultural policy   health
economic and social cohesion   social policy
education   transport
employment   vocational training
environment   youth policy

When the body was first formed, there was some hope that it might come to resemble a second chamber, working alongside the European Parliament. The European Parliament was reluctant to share any of its newly acquired powers, however. The idea of this regional upper chamber was dropped.

What the Committee of Regions tries to do is to bring the European Union closer to the people. By having representatives from regional and local government, they also bring the people closer to the European Union. Much policy implementation is carried out at the regional or local level. Therefore, it seems sensible to have local and regional input.

The Economic and Social Committee

Unlike the Committee of Regions, the **Economic and Social Committee** was not created in the Treaty of European Union. Its existence dates back to the Treaty of Rome. Its role has been adapted by the various treaties, however, including the Treaty of European Union and the Treaty of Nice. The number of delegates from each member state is identical to that of the Committee of Regions, but the representatives are all unelected and are appointed by the national governments. The Economic and Social Committee comprises representatives from three different groups: employers, employees and various interest or pressure groups. Each of the three groups is similar in size. Of its twenty-four members, Britain contributes nine to the employers group, eight to the employees group, and seven to the various interests.

The employers are drawn from the public and the private sectors. Professions include commerce, trade, transport and agriculture. From the British delegation, there are private business people, bankers, and staff from the Women's National Commission. The employees are mostly drawn from trade unions, most of which are affiliated to the European Trade Union Confederation. All members from Britain have a trade-union background. The unions cover the public and the private sectors. The group of various interests covers all aspects of life, excluding those covered by the first two groups. This would also include environmental groups and consumer organisations. It works to highlight cultural or social issues, some of which might not be within the ambit of the two other groups. One of the British members works for the Runnymede Trust. Another works for the Royal Bank of Scotland Centre for the Older Person's Agenda (see Table 9.6). These issues are not really covered in the other two groups.

As with the Committee of Regions, the Economic and Social Committee is an advisory body. Its claim is, however, that it draws in experts from the different aspects of social and economic life – acknowledging that elected politicians and civil servants are not always experts. The input that can be given by this Committee draws in aspects of life that may not be covered in any of the other EU institutions. This makes it a valuable asset to the Commission when drawing up legislative proposals. Arguably, the Economic and Social Committee is a supranational organisation. It may be appointed by national governments but the way in which it operates goes far beyond national self-interest.

The European Ombudsman

The European Ombudsman was created in the Treaty of European Union. During the treaty negotiations, Britain was one of the member states most enthusiastic about creating such a body. It came into being in 1995. The current European Ombudsman is Professor Nikiforos Diamandouros who has been in post since 2003.

The idea of the Ombudsman was to help bring the European Union closer to the people. The Ombudsman investigates *maladministration*. Although this is a very difficult term to define, it is broadly to do with the way in which policies are implemented. It is not to do with whether a policy is good or bad but simply about how that policy has been applied. Investigations can cover any part of the EU although it has been the Commission that has been most frequently investigated. In 2003, over 70 per cent of complaints were about the Commission.

Box 3.2 Complaining to the Ombudsman

In 2002, a guide to the Ombudsman was published. It explained when you could complain to the Ombudsman:

> If an institution fails to do something it should have done, if it does it in the wrong way or if it does something it should not have done, there may be reason to complain to the Ombudsman. Some of the most common problems he deals with are unnecessary delay, refusal of information, discrimination and abuse of power.[1]

What makes the European Ombudsman an interesting body is that it can initiate its own enquiries. This must be to do with the EU, however. National concerns are beyond the remit of the European Ombudsman. This ability to start investigations gives the Ombudsman far more power than the Court of Justice which must be *asked* to investigate any concerns within its remit. Decisions by the Ombudsman, particularly when proving maladministration, tend to be followed through and addressed. It is very rare for this not to occur. Should such a circumstance arise, then the Ombudsman will write a special report to the European Parliament. This is the ultimate weapon of the Ombudsman but it is then left to the European Parliament to follow up the report. It becomes a political issue rather than an administrative one.

The 'democratic deficit'

When examining the different institutions of the European Union, one of the most noticeable things is that almost all of them are unelected. The only body which is directly elected is the European Parliament. Members of the Council of Ministers and the Committee of Regions may have been elected to national, regional or local bodies, and could be considered to be indirectly elected. The vast majority of posts are appointed.

To make matters worse, there is little transparency in how each of the institutions functions, and how they can be held to account. The European Parliament and the European Ombudsman can try to hold other institutions to account but there is always the possibility that they might be overruled by the Council of Ministers or the European Council.

The lack of transparency, together with the limited opportunities to hold the different institutions to account via direct elections, have led to accusations that the European Union suffers from a **democratic deficit**. Even with the European Parliament acting as a co-decision maker, there is still limited opportunity for the general public to become involved with the EU. The idea of a democracy in very simple terms is that the people rule. Normally, this would mean our elected representatives govern. As the European Parliament is not a proper legislature, however, there is negligible opportunity for the people to 'rule'.

Arguably, with the creation of the Committee of Regions and the continuing role of the Economic and Social Committee, steps have been taken to draw in different aspects of society into the policy process. It could be argued, however, that these committees represent vested interests and that the general public is still ignored.

A counter-argument to this is the lack of interest shown by the public when they are given the opportunity to vote in the direct elections to the European Parliament. Turnout in many countries is woefully poor. The United Kingdom turnout in the 2004 elections was 38.8 per cent – which was a vast improvement on the 24 per cent turnout in 1999. Yet across the EU as a whole, the turnout in 2004 was 45.6 per cent. Belgium had the highest turnout, with 90.8 per cent, followed by Luxembourg, Malta and Italy. The poorest turnout was in Slovakia (16.9 per cent), followed by Poland and Estonia. Only seven of the twenty-five member states had a turnout greater than 50 per cent. Therefore, drawing in other non-elected persons via the Economic and Social Committee, and locally and regionally elected representatives via the Committee of Regions, may be the only way to address the democratic deficit in the short term.

In the longer term, there is a real need for the European Union to address the democratic deficit. The problem is how to do so? Making people aware of what the EU does could be one way forward. The Ombudsman has used this approach and, as a result, there have been many more complaints about the lack of transparency in the EU. The greater number of complaints may not be solely to do with the problems of the EU but also to do with a greater awareness of the European Ombudsman system.

The problem is how to publicise such success stories? Most mass media are unlikely to publish or broadcast such news. It is bad news that makes news. In Britain, stories such as banning British sausages or banning bent cucumbers are more likely to be seen or heard than EU investments into the British infrastructure. Thus it is likely that the democratic deficit will remain.

••

✔ What you should have learnt from reading this chapter

- The different institutions of the European Union have clear roles to play. There is some overlap between them. They are also all mutually dependent upon one another.

- The most important institutions within the European Union are the Council of Ministers, the European Council, the Commission, the Court of Justice and the European Parliament.

- There is much concern that the European Union suffers from a 'democratic deficit'. Only one institution is directly elected – the European Parliament. All the others are appointed. Added to this, there is great concern that the different EU institutions are very difficult to hold to account. Some of this is to do with the lack of elections, but also because of the lack of transparency in their operations.

- To counter the accusations of a 'democratic deficit', a number of bodies has been drawn into the policy-making process – the Committee of Regions and the Economic and Social Committee. The problem here is that these bodies are purely consultative. The European Parliament is now a 'co-decision-maker'. By giving it a more prominent and more influential role, it is hoped that the accusation of 'democratic deficit' will be diminished.

- The British role in each of these bodies is significant. As the European Union becomes larger, it gets more difficult to protect national interests should they conflict with those of the EU. By working with representatives from other member states, however, British representatives can promote policies that will benefit the entire EU.

Glossary of key terms

Co-decision The power of co-decision means that the European Parliament and the Council of Ministers have become almost equal partners in the legislative process of the European Union. In effect, the European Parliament is consulted on three occasions (similar to the three readings of a bill in the British House of Commons) on legislative proposals. If the opinions of the European Parliament are not accepted, the Council of Ministers is now compelled to explain its reasoning. The Council of Ministers must also be unanimous in its rejection of the advice of the European Parliament.

Commission This body is sometimes perceived as the civil service of the EU, although it is far more important. The Commission draws up legislative proposals for consideration by other EU institutions – most notably the Council of Ministers and the European Parliament. The Commission is also the Guardian of the Treaties. This means that the Commission tries to make sure that all member states uphold both the letter and the spirit of the agreements made in key treaties (such as the Treaty of Rome, Treaty of European Union, etc.). Commissioners are appointed by national governments although they are supposed to work to further the aims of the EU, *not* national aims. The European Parliament has to approve the Commission before the commissioners enter their posts.

Committee of Regions An advisory body created by the Treaty of European Union. Delegates come from regional and local government from all member states. The Committee of Regions must be consulted in a number of specified policy areas, although its advice is just that and need not be heeded. The existence of this body, however, highlights the importance of regionalism and subsidiarity to the EU.

Council of Ministers/Council of the European Union The Council of Ministers is considered to be the most important body within the EU. In effect, it is the lawmaking body of the EU although it is now a co-decision maker with the European Parliament. When the Council of Ministers meets, each member state sends a representative. Thus, when agriculture is under discussion, each member state will send their Minister of Agriculture; when the issue is transport, the Transport Ministers will attend, etc. Decisions can be taken by simple majority, qualified majority or unanimity

Court of First Instance This body was created in 1988 to assist the Court of Justice. The Court of First Instance deals with matters of fact, as opposed to legal interpretation. It now works independently of the Court of Justice. Its membership is currently made up of twenty-five judges, one from each member state.

Court of Justice The role of the Court of Justice is as a final court of appeal. It also makes sure that all member states uphold the treaties that have formed the EU. It is not proactive, which means that it must be asked to investigate a particular issue. The Court of Justice deals with matters of law, as opposed to matters of fact. There are twenty-five judges, one from each member state, assisted by eight advocates-general.

Democratic deficit This is a difficult term to explain although, at a basic level, it suggests a lack of democracy. This could be because there is little or no electoral accountability, or that there is a lack of transparency in the decision-making process – which again suggests a lack of accountability to the people.

Economic and Social Committee An unelected body which draws in people from different aspects of economic and social life: employers, employees and pressure groups. It is a consultative body and its opinions are not binding.

European Council This body is sometimes considered to be the upper tier of the Council of Ministers although it is not actually part of the Council of Ministers. It comprises the various heads of government, and has the power to overrule the Council of Ministers and the European Parliament.

European Parliament This is the only directly elected institution in the European Union. The European Parliament is a 'co-decision maker' with the Council of Ministers. This means that the European Parliament has a significant input into the legislative process of the EU, although its opinions can still be overruled by the Council of Ministers or the European Council. The European Parliament also has a power of veto over the budget and over appointments to the Commission. In both cases it is a case of accept or reject in entirety.

Qualified Majority Voting (QMV) This system is used for much decision making in the Council of Ministers. Each member state is given a specified number of votes, dependent upon the population size of the country. At the time of writing, using QMV, to get a policy proposal passed requires 232 out of 321 votes. Alternatively, ninety votes are needed to block a proposal.

Sovereignty This is the right of a state to pass laws within its own territory. It is suggested that EU membership undermines national sovereignty as all members have to cede a range of powers to the EU. Added to this, EU law overrides national law when the two conflict.

Subsidiarity This is the process of devolving decision-making down to the most appropriate tier of government. At its most basic level, the aim of subsidiarity was to take decision-making away from the EU and return it to national governments. Some aspects of subsidiarity, however, could see decision-making being devolved to regional or local government.

? Likely examination questions

Why is the label 'democratic deficit' used when describing the European Union? To what extent, if at all, is this label justified?

Evaluate ways in which the powers of the European Parliament could be increased. What are the major obstacles to such moves?

'The Commission is still the powerhouse behind the development of the EU.' Discuss.

Successive British governments have been eager to make the European Union more open and more transparent. Evaluate the extent to which they have achieved such aims.

Helpful websites

There is a number of useful websites for the different EU institutions:

curia.eu.int/en/transitpage.htm is the web page that leads to the European Court of Justice, the Court of First Instance and other information about EU law in Europe.

www.cor.eu.int/en/index.htm is the homepage for the Committee of Regions.

www.esc.eu.int/index_en.asp is the homepage of the Economic and Social Committee. From here you can look at the three different groups in the Committee.

www.euro-ombudsman.eu.int/home/en/default.htm is the homepage of the European Ombudsman. From here you can access information about the powers of the Ombudsman as well as annual reports.

www.europarl.eu.int is the homepage of the European Parliament.

www.europarl.org.uk/index.htm is the British homepage of the European Parliament. Here you can find much information about British MEPs and their roles in the European Parliament. All of the election results going back to 1979 are included here as well.

europa.eu.int/comm./index_en.htm is the homepage of the Commission. From here you can find information about current issues, policies and staff of the Commission.

ue.eu.int/cms3_fo/showPage.asp?id=242&lang=en&mode=g is the homepage of the Council of Ministers (also known as the Council of the European Union). From here it is also possible to access the Council of Europe.

Suggestions for further reading

D. Bostock, 'Coreper Revisited', *Journal of Common Market Studies*, vol. 40, no. 2 (2002) pp. 215–34.

L. Cram, D. Dinan and N. Nugent (eds), *Developments in the European Union* (Palgrave, 1999) contains a number of chapters on the different institutions of the EU.

R. Delhousse, *The European Court of Justice* (Palgrave, 1994).

F. Hayes-Renshaw and H. Wallace, *The Council of Ministers* (Palgrave, 2006) 2nd edition.

A. Jones, 'UK Relations with the EU; and Did You Notice the Elections?', *Talking Politics*, vol. 12, no. 2 (2000) pp. 312–17.

D. Judge and D. Earnshaw, *The European Parliament* (Palgrave, 2003).

N. Nugent, *The European Commission* (Palgrave, 2001).

J. Peterson and M. Shackleton (eds), *The Institutions of the European Union* (Oxford University Press, 2002).

J. Tallberg, 'The Power of the Presidency: Brokerage, Efficiency and Distribution in EU Negotiations', *Journal of Common Market Studies*, vol. 42, no. 5 (2004) pp. 999–1022.

CHAPTER 4

Common Policies of the European Union

Contents

Overview

Though seen as controversial, the common policies of the European Union are an important feature of the organisation. The best known is the Common Agricultural Policy (CAP), yet there are others, including Fisheries, and Foreign and Security. For the most part, attitudes in Britain towards these common policies are anything but positive. Yet many of the criticisms may appear unjust. The problem is not necessarily the common policies but rather the way in which they have, or have not, developed to suit the modern era. For example, one of the aims of the CAP was to make Europe self-sufficient in food production. This was in an era prior to genetically modified crops or the industrialisation of agriculture. The aim was – and still is – worthy but the way in which the CAP is structured may need reconsideration. This chapter will examine the origins and development of a number of common policies, with British perspectives on each being evaluated.

Key issues to be covered in this chapter

- The origins and development of the Common Agricultural Policy, along with an analysis of the current reforms
- The problems with developing the Common Fisheries Policy
- The aims and objectives of the Competition Policy will be evaluated. This will be done in conjunction with the idea of the free market. Therefore, trade policy will also need to be assessed
- How the Common Foreign and Security Policy has been developed, along with its current aims and objectives
- The development of the single currency will be evaluated, along with its predecessors
- An evaluation of the British position on each of these common policies

Why have common policies?

In the modern world, the idea of developing a common policy and then applying it to twenty-five different countries seems a little peculiar. This is even more so when a central body funds such policies. Yet the development of common policies has been a feature in the advance of the European Union. Such common policies are utilised around the world – although they are not necessarily labelled as such. The vast majority of countries makes use of the free market, and there are rules and regulations which they have to follow. These are policed by bodies such as the World Trade Organisation (WTO).

Within the EU, there are particular areas of policy where the EU has the 'competence'. This means that the EU is responsible for developing policies in this area rather than the individual member states doing so; an example of this would be agriculture. At the same time, there are other competences, such as social security, which come within the remit of national governments. Each country can develop its own benefits system.

Where the EU is the chief policy-maker, the idea is to get all member states to work towards the goals being set by the EU. One of the easier ways of doing this is to develop a common policy platform. This may be done via the development of an EU treaty, and can then be applied to all member states. Yet there are times and particular policy areas where this may not be feasible. In such circumstances a **common position** may be developed instead. Either way, the EU sets the parameters in which all the member states have to operate, unless an opt-out has been negotiated. For example, Britain, Denmark and Sweden opted out of joining the euro.

The Common Agricultural Policy

The **Common Agricultural Policy (CAP)** was actually part of the Treaty of Rome (1957) which laid the foundations for the formation of the European Economic Community. The aims and objectives of the CAP are detailed in Box 4.1. It was not until January 1962, however, that the CAP came into being.

Box 4.1 The principles and instruments of the Common Agricultural Policy

Article 39 of the Treaty of Rome laid down the key points of the CAP:

1. to increase agricultural productivity by promoting technical progress and by ensuring the rational development of agricultural production;
2. to ensure a fair standard of living for the agricultural community, in particular, by increasing the individual earnings of persons working in agriculture;
3. to stabilise markets;
4. to ensure the availability of supplies;
5. to ensure that the supplies reach the consumers at reasonable prices.

Actually to make the CAP work, the original six member states of the EEC had to develop a single market in agriculture. Linked to this there were to be common prices across all member states, and free trade in agricultural goods between the six member states. Without such market unity, the policy would be doomed to failure.

What the CAP tried to do – and was successful in doing so – was to guarantee minimum prices for farmers. Rather than the market setting the prices, the EEC would fix the prices centrally. If prices fell below a certain level, surpluses would be bought up by the EEC to keep the prices at a reasonable level.

Linked to this development of market unity was the idea of **community preference**. Given a choice between an agricultural product from the EEC and a non-EEC equivalent, all EEC member states would be expected to buy the Community product. To make sure this happened, non-EEC competitors were able to enter the market only at a predetermined price. In other words, tariff barriers were set up around the EEC to protect it from external competition. It would be impossible for a flood of cheaper agricultural imports to enter the market. This system kept agricultural prices higher but was done to make sure that farmers had a reasonable income. There was a fear that, if agricultural incomes were not high enough, many people might leave their jobs in the agricultural sector to find work elsewhere. A consequence of this could be that the EEC would then become dependent upon imports of food. Such a situation had existed in the immediate aftermath of World War II, where there had been severe food shortages which had left many Europeans starving. There was no way that the EEC was going to let such conditions ever happen again. To ensure this was the case, the EEC aimed to become self-sufficient in food production.

All this expenditure on agriculture came from a specific source: the **European Agricultural Guidance and Guarantee Fund (EAGGF)**. There were two parts to this fund – guidance, and guarantee. As its name suggested, the guarantee section covered the costs in the market system. It was the more important part in that it guaranteed the minimum income, and was classified as compulsory expenditure. This meant that its funding came from the EEC budget. Between 1999 and 2002, Britain was the fifth largest recipient of funds from the guarantee section out of the fifteen member states at that time. The guidance aspect was to do with the structural funds – guiding the development and possible reform of the agricultural sector. The United Kingdom was again one of the largest recipients of such funding, being the sixth or seventh largest recipient between 1999 and 2002.

The impact of the CAP was phenomenal. Agricultural production rose to the extent that the EEC started to produce more than was required – this is termed **overproduction**. Today, the European Union is self-sufficient in almost every aspect of food production (of products grown in the EU). For example, in the year 2000, the EU was more than self-sufficient in cereals, beef meat, and wine. Even in products such as olive oil and sugar beet, the EU had a self-sufficiency rating of over 99 per cent.

There have been seemingly endless calls for the reform of the CAP. Even the Luxembourg Compromise (see chapter 2) had its origins in a dispute over the reform of the CAP. One of the major reasons has been that of cost. As a percentage of the budget, the CAP has always taken a huge proportion. This has been heightened by the percentage of the workforce actually employed in the agricultural sector. In 2003, for the fifteen EU states at the time, it was around 5 per cent of the collective workforce.

A major concern for many states – and Britain has been to the forefront here – has been the reform of the CAP. One aspect, in particular,

Table 4.1 Budgetary expenditure on the Common Agricultural Policy (€ millions)[1]

	2000	2001	2002	2003	2004
Total EU budget	77,878.8	101,051.0	95,656.4	97,502.9	100,675.9
EAGGF – Guarantee	40,466.7	42,083.3	43,214.3	44,780.5	44,760.4
EAGGF – Guidance	1,387.3	3,508.9	2,969.9	3,122.7	3,564.7
Other agricultural spending	49.1	49.8	55.3	42.1	35.4
Total agricultural spending	41,903.1	45,642.0	46,239.5	47,945.3	48,360.5
Agricultural spending as a percentage of total EU Budget	53.81	45.17	48.34	49.17	48.04

has been cost. When Britain joined the EEC in 1973, the CAP took up around 90 per cent of the budget. This has been reduced over time, as can be seen in Table 4.1, to the extent that the CAP now takes up around half the budget. Yet the concern is that half of the budget is being spent on less than 5 per cent of the EU workforce (prior to enlargement in 2004). The agricultural output contributes around 2.4 per cent of the total EU gross domestic product (GDP). It is hardly surprising that there have been so many calls for reform.

There have been steps taken to reform the CAP, although it is argued by some that much more is needed. The 1972 Mansholt reforms (proposed by the then Commissioner for Agriculture, Sicco Mansholt) introduced the Guidance aspect of the EAGGF. This directed a small amount of funding away from guaranteeing funds for farmers to providing some funds to restructure agriculture. As can be seen in Table 4.1, however, even today the amount of money made available for the Guidance aspect of the EAGGF is very small indeed.

What has been noticeable with the CAP is that the large farms and the wealthy farmers have all done exceedingly well out of the CAP. In 2004, the Queen received over half a million pounds from the CAP, Prince Charles almost £700,000, and the Duke of Westminster received almost £500,000. The largest recipient of funding from the CAP was Sir Richard Sutton who received over £1 million in subsidies. Big businesses in Britain did even better, with Tate & Lyle receiving around £220 million over the two-year period 2003–4. In the same time period, Nestlé received around £30 million.

In the early 1990s, Ray MacSharry introduced plans to reform the agricultural support systems. He proposed replacing the guarantee funds with a form of income support. This idea was known as **decoupling**, where the relationship between production and funding would be reduced. This was a move from price support to income support. Such a proposal caused a furore within some member states of the EU. The farmers involved, however, received generous payments to make up for any shortfall in income. One aspect that received some support was in taking land out of agricultural production. Farmers were given the opportunity to set aside 15 per cent of their land. The idea was to reduce the overproduction of some crops. Any farmers involved were compensated for their loss of income – in fact, the compensation led to an increase in running costs for the CAP even though it reduced output.

More recently, there were the **Agenda 2000** reforms, which were published in July 1997 and eventually agreed in March 1999. The plans included further cuts to the price supports, especially in beef, milk and cereals. Again there was generous compensation for farmers. There were also moves to improve the rural environment and to protect the rural heritage. Around 10 per cent of CAP funding was set aside for such schemes. Added to this, Agenda 2000 attempted to increase competition between farmers in the hope of forcing prices down. Finally, there were issues of food quality and food safety. A European Food Safety Authority was established in 2002. Part of this involved making feed and food operators aware of their responsibilities, as well as increased surveillance of the operators. All of the Agenda 2000 plans actually led to increased spending on the CAP.

In June 2003, further decoupling was introduced. Also the support for farmers was changed. Each farm would receive a single payment.

This was to be dependent upon the size of the farm and the amount of subsidy received between 2000 and 2002. There were a host of other requirements, including set-aside.

While there have been these reforms, there has still been pressure from beyond the EU for further reform to the CAP. It is argued that the CAP undermines both free trade and open competition. The United States, in particular, demands that the CAP be reformed, while conveniently ignoring the subsidy of US agriculture. Countries such as New Zealand, which have very little state subsidy of agriculture, have also been prominent in demanding reforms. The EU has moved slowly in meeting these demands while, at the same time, requesting similar reforms from its competitors – most notably the United States.

What has really stimulated reform of the CAP has been the enlargement process. With ten new members joining in 2004, the vast majority of EU states acknowledged the urgent need for reform. With eight of the ten new member states likely to be very heavily dependent upon agricultural subsidies, it appeared that the CAP would bankrupt the European Union. These agricultural supports for the new member states were phased in gradually while, at the same time, more aspects of the CAP were reformed. This was not to the liking of the new member states.

While examining the CAP, there seems to be a notion that there is a common EU position on the policy. That is anything but the case. Within the EU there are clear divisions between member states that wish to have a radical overhaul of the CAP and those that want it to remain largely unchanged. Britain, for example, is in the former camp, France the latter. During the British presidency of the EU in the second half of 2005, attempts were made by the Blair government to reform CAP funding, as part of a total overhaul of the EU budget. In this, Blair was generally seen to be unsuccessful.

The Department of the Environment, Food and Rural Affairs (DEFRA), however, has published a paper on how it views the development of the CAP over the next ten to fifteen years. This paper, entitled 'A Vision for the Common Agricultural Policy', was published in December 2005. It looks to the development of a sustainable model for the future of EU agriculture. There is a range of different areas that are evaluated, including the quality of food being produced, the removal of subsidies, the welfare of livestock, and the importance of trade. An examination of what reforms are needed (from the British perspective, although the language used suggests a European one) is also presented. The economic, social and environmental costs of the current situation, and of any reforms, are taken into consideration.

The British position is quite clear. The CAP spends too much money, and should be removed. The cost to the EU is estimated at around €100 billion for the period 2007–13. Much of this money could be better spent elsewhere. The subsidies distort world trade, and keep many of the world's poorest countries in a state of under-development.

In the short term, it appears unlikely that the member states which benefit from the CAP will be enthusiastic about DEFRA's suggestions. As the new member states (those who joined in 2004) will receive their full share of CAP monies by 2014, however, it is likely that some major reforms will occur before then. Current beneficiaries of the CAP (such as France, Spain, Portugal, Ireland and Greece) will see their CAP receipts diminish – possibly to the extent that they may become net contributors to the EU budget! If there is no further reform of the CAP, there are suggestions that the EU may not be able to afford to pay all the CAP subsidies.

The Common Fisheries Policy

The **Common Fisheries Policy** is one of the least evaluated of the European Union's common policies. One of the reasons for this is that it affects a very small percentage of the EU workforce – 0.2 per cent. It also contributes less than 1 per cent to the overall EU gross domestic prodcuct. Bearing in mind that 'fish and chips' is still considered to be one of Britain's favourite meals, however, you would think that there would be more interest in this policy.

The Common Fisheries Policy came into being in 1983. Prior to this, there had been common positions developed on fishing, dating back to the early 1970s. The fishing industry has been quite resentful of the amount of money spent on agriculture. There were expectations that the Common Fisheries Policy would deliver similar wealth to the fishing industry. This has not been the case. What the Common Fisheries Policy has attempted to do is settle issues such as territorial fishing rights and the amount of fish caught by each member state.

The rationale behind the Common Fisheries Policy is quite simple. There are three components:

to ensure fishing stocks are not overexploited;
to care for the marine ecosystem;
to protect the interests of fishermen and of consumers.

Within this rationale, there is a number of clear policy areas. An overview of these is presented in Box 4.2. The Common Fisheries Policy has been able to resolve some differences between national fishing fleets. For example, there has been trouble between the Spanish, on the one hand, and the British and French on the other. When Spain was not in the then European Community, there was a lot of concern over Spanish boats fishing in EC waters – the Spanish fleet was as big as that of the EC. The negotiations for Spanish accession to the EC included specific detailed negotiations on fishing.

Box 4.2 The policy areas of the Common Fisheries Policy

1. Access and conservation

   - EU 200-mile zone for all EU fishermen
   - 12-mile limit on own shores for member states
   - all conservation levels to be agreed at the EU level
   - national quotas established to protect fish stocks. These are known as **total allowable catches (TACs)**

2. Market management

   - price system
   - marketing arrangements
   - external trade policy

3. Structural measures
   funding is available from the EU budget, for

   - processing and marketing development projects
   - conversion and modernisation schemes
   - redeployment

4. External negotiations

   - negotiations with non-EU states on fishing, and in particular on access to EU waters

The original idea for the Common Fisheries Policy was that it would be renewed after twenty years. Thus the policy was renegotiated from 2002, resulting in a new version of the policy in 2003.

One of the problems for the Common Fisheries Policy is that it is very difficult to police. Short of having someone on every single boat

Box 4.3 Key points from the Common Fisheries Policy Review (2003)

1. Sustainable development of European **aquaculture**

   - aquaculture is the creation or rearing of aquatic organisms
   - increase production beyond the natural capacity
   - development of fish farming and mollusc farming

2. Environmental protection integrated into Common Fisheries Policy

   - idea of 'polluter pays'
   - precaution, prevention and rectification of pollution
   - reduce pressure on fishing grounds
   - protect all wildlife from the adverse effects of fishing

3. Eradication of illegal fishing

   - priority concern
   - better monitoring of fishing

4. Measures to counter fleet restructuring

   - focus on social, economic and regional consequences
   - bilateral consultation with member states
   - use of structural funds to alleviate the situation

5. Reduction of discards

   - 'discards' are fish (or crustaceans or molluscs) which are caught by fishing equipment but then thrown back into the sea
   - analyse the reasons for discards
   - assess the consequences of discards

6. Creation of a single inspection structure

   - new legal framework for Community control and enforcement system
   - member states and the EU are both to be given clearly defined roles in the monitoring process, as well as enforcement

to monitor all catches, it is almost impossible to know how much fish is actually being caught.

The 2003 version of the Common Fisheries Policy places great emphasis upon sustainable development in fishing, protecting the environment, and eradicating illegal practices. This is detailed in Box 4.3. It shows how much breadth there is now in the Common Fisheries Policy. As with the CAP, there is now far greater emphasis upon environmental issues as well.

From a British perspective, the Common Fisheries Policy has appeared to have had a detrimental effect upon the British industry. Around half of the British 'white fish' fleet has been tied up. Those boats which are still fishing have had their time at sea reduced by half. On top of this, there are stringent restrictions on the national quotas, which contribute to the overall EU Total Allowable Catches. In December 2005, there was a 15 per cent cut in the size of the quotas for cod, herring and whiting, and a 13 per cent cut for haddock. At the same time, there were increases in the quota of North Sea prawns (30 per cent), monkfish caught in the Irish Sea (5 per cent) and a 3 per cent increase for hake. The feeling from the British government was (at this time) that there had been a turnaround in the fish stocks and that the cuts, particularly in cod, would soon be reversed. Those in the fishing industry, however, simply saw more cuts in the British quotas and the possible death of the British fishing industry. The overall cod catch had been cut by 65 per cent in the previous three years, and the cuts were continuing.

Part of the problem is that the fishing industry in Britain disputes the figures provided by the EU and conservation groups for the size of fishing stocks. For example, the EU produced figures to show that, in 2000, the amount of mature cod in the North Sea was about 60,000 tonnes, compared to almost 200,000 in 1983, and that the stocks are still shrinking. The British fishing industry has produced evidence that stocks are actually increasing, and have been doing so for a number of years. As a result, there have been calls from the British fishing industry to scrap the Common Fisheries Policy.

Competition Policy and Trade Policy

Competition Policy and Trade Policy are closely linked. A third area that is also closely related is the **Common Commercial**

Policy. Each of these also has a profound impact upon other common policies, particularly the CAP.

Competition Policy and the Common Commercial Policy have their origins in the Treaty of Rome. In fact, the Competition Policy can also be seen in the Treaty of Paris. Within the Treaty of Rome, it is Article 113 that is important. It focuses upon a common tariff and common trade agreements with third countries. The common tariff requires a single market to operate effectively. A single market was in existence from 1968 but it was after the signing of the Single European Act (SEA) that both Competition Policy and the Common Commercial Policy grew in importance.

The aim of the Competition Policy is to prevent distortions in competition caused by private firms or by government actions. Thus there are two parts to the policy: (a) activities of the private sector; and (b) the activities of the state or state-sponsored sector. While the EEC – and later the EU – could propose ways in which these distortions could be prevented, the reality was that all this was complementary to national governmental action. As the EU has developed, however, these national principles on competition have moved into alignment with those of the EU. Ultimately, this can be seen as a stepping stone in the integration process of the EU.

The Competition Policy is also applicable externally, that is, beyond the EU. The principles behind the Competition Policy (which are examined below) are built into many of the trade agreements that the EU constructs with non-EU members. This has been a cause for much concern, particularly for the United States which sees these principles as undermining free-market ideals.

Competition Policy covers a wide range of issues. It tries to prevent the abuse of a dominant market position. This is where a single business may have little or no competition and is therefore in a position to charge whatever price it likes for the goods or service that it provides. The Competition Policy can be used to prevent such an organisation from overcharging its customers. It can also be used to prevent businesses from attempting to eliminate their competition by deliberately undercharging for their products. Even mergers between businesses may be prevented under Competition Policy if they are likely to have an adverse effect for consumers or for competition in that area of business.

Another area is the problem of cartels. This is where a group of companies from different countries get together and rig prices. As a result, consumers would have to pay higher prices for the goods or service provided. Under the Competition Policy, such actions are not permitted.

The Competition Policy can also be used to prevent governments from undermining competition. For example, if a country passes laws that restrict which businesses may compete for a government tender to businesses from that country, this goes against the idea of open, free and fair competition. Under Competition Policy rules, national monopolies may also be opened up to competition, especially if they are inefficient.

The Common Commercial Policy originally focused upon the common external tariff and quotas of goods entering the EEC/EU. This remit has widened over time, however, and is now much more widespread. Areas covered by the Common Commercial Policy now include regulatory issues such as product conformity. The idea here is to make sure that products entering the EU market conform to such things as EU safety standards. Added to this, the emphasis is also moving away from trade in goods to trade in services, which is a lot more difficult to monitor. This is further complicated by the growing importance of issues such as the environment, as well as the continuing development of technology.

The Commission plays a key role in competition, commercial and trade policies. For organisations that break the Competition Policy guidelines, it is the Commission that will try to persuade the organisation to change its methods. If this is unsuccessful, then the Commission can order the organisation to change, and can even fine it as well. In many respects, with regard to the breaking of Competition Policy, the Commission can be seen as prosecutor, judge and jury. There is, however, a right of appeal for the organisation. Such an appeal would be dealt by the Court of First Instance (see chapter 3).

Under the Common Commercial Policy, the Commission has been given the power to negotiate with third parties on trade deals, and so on, but any decisions proposed by the Commission must be approved by the Council of Ministers. This makes trade negotiations with the EU very cumbersome. A recent example of such problems was the trade dispute between the EU and China in 2005. A deal was reached by the Trade Commissioner, Peter Mandelson, but it had to be approved by the Council of Ministers – and some member states were not very happy with the deal that had been negotiated.

One of the big issues about the Common Commercial Policy and the Competition Policy is that they do not seem to fit in with the ideas of the CAP. Competition Policy places an emphasis on trade liberalisation – which, among other things, is meant to ensure that the internal market is not distorted. It also highlights that state aid distorts competition. On the issue of state aid, the Competition Policy states: 'By giving certain firms or products favoured treatment to the detriment of other firms or products, state aid seriously disrupts normal competitive forces.'[2] Arguably, the subsidies given to farmers via the CAP seriously disrupt normal competitive forces. Some state aid is permitted, however, and there is a number of areas under which the CAP might therefore be exempt, including: important projects of common European interest; and the development of certain areas.

Britain's position on Competition Policy and the Common Commercial Policy is broadly supportive. The British government, along with the Netherlands and many East European states, is a strong supporter of trade liberalisation. The idea of state subsidies undermines the free market, and they should be removed. Competition should be open, free and fair. In this respect, Britain sees many benefits for all EU members through trade liberalisation and a reduction in dependency upon the state. This perspective is fundamentally different from that of the French government which is very much in favour of protectionist policies. The EU ends up trying to strike a balance between these diametrically opposed positions.

The Common Foreign and Security Policy

Developing a common policy in the areas of foreign affairs and security has proved to be rather difficult. In 1969, at the Hague summit, the idea of **European political co-operation (EPC)** was established. This came into effect in 1970. The idea was to develop a consensus on foreign policy, based around intergovernmental co-operation. All this was established outside of the framework of the EEC. There were no votes on any issues, nor were any decisions binding. Added to this, military and security matters were omitted. Despite all this, the aim was to develop a common position on foreign affairs.

Although EPC was formalised under the Single European Act, it was its evolution into the **Common Foreign and Security Policy (CFSP)** – as part of the Treaty of European Union – that saw a huge step forward in co-operation between member states on foreign matters.

The aim of the CFSP is, like EPC, to encourage co-operation between member states on foreign policy. Where this co-operation is achieved, the idea is that it will lead to joint action by member states. The problem is that the CFSP is not really a proper 'common policy'. In all of the other common policies cited in this chapter, there is a pooling of responsibilities by the member states, and it is all co-ordinated by the Commission. In the case of CFSP, there is no pooling of resources, and the decision-making process is led by the Council of Ministers. Rather than being a supranational agreement, CFSP is still very much intergovernmental. Even the language used in the policy is very loose, especially when compared with other common policies. There are phrases such as 'common values', 'fundamental interest', and 'to preserve peace and stability'. Yet, despite all this, there has been some movement towards a more co-ordinated approach to foreign policy by EU member states.

There was always a number of problems with the CFSP. One of these was the issue of neutrality. Countries such as Ireland and Sweden have maintained that they are neutral states that do not get involved in wars. This has made it very difficult to develop a common position, especially when unanimity was required on any decisions made.

The unanimous decision-making was changed in the Treaty of Amsterdam (1999). Instead of unanimity, there were two alternatives:

1. constructive abstention;
2. emergency brake.

Constructive abstention provided the opportunity for member states to 'not support' a particular policy proposal under CFSP. Under the rules of unanimity, the options were 'support' or 'oppose'. Constructive abstention enables up to one-third of member states to abstain without defeating the policy proposal.

Under the emergency brake, decisions are taken under qualified majority voting. If a member state wishes to veto a decision, however, it is referred to the European Council. Should this happen the European Council has to operate under unanimity. This gives all member states the opportunity to rethink their positions. Should a proposal go this far, it is unlikely to be passed.

While there has been gradual convergence on foreign policy decision-making under CFSP, there has been a number of problems. The troubles in the Balkans and Kosovo in the 1990s highlighted the difficulty in getting all member states to agree on a decision – and that was only with twelve and fifteen member states. Decision-making on Iraq was just as bad, with the United States pouring proverbial fuel on the flames when Donald Rumsfeld talked about there being a 'new' Europe and an 'old' Europe. The 'new' Europe consisted of the newer member states of the EU, and the United Kingdom, and these governments were broadly supportive of the US intervention in Iraq.

Yet, despite these setbacks, the idea that CFSP is evolving and developing still holds some truth. In Helsinki in December 1999, there was a move to establish a European Rapid Reaction Force as part of a **European Security and Defence Policy (ESDP)**. This ESDP is under the CFSP. Not only does it focus on security and defence, but also on humanitarian aid and peacekeeping. The **Rapid Reaction Force** is sometimes perceived as a putative European army. Yet it is not. Most EU member states acknowledge the primacy of NATO in their defence policies. The Rapid Reaction Force is likely to work alongside NATO, enabling the European Union to increase its global role without seemingly being tied to American apron strings.

The British position on CFSP has been interesting. At all times, the British government has argued that NATO is paramount. Any developments in the CFSP are not to be at the expense of NATO. There have been fears expressed that CFSP will lead to Britain being dragged by our European partners into wars about which we know nothing. Other fears were that CFSP would lead to a Common Defence Policy and the development of a European army. All British troops would then be under the control of the European Union. Yet, there is no European army, nor would Britain relinquish control of British troops to the EU.

Despite the expression of such fears, Britain has been to the forefront in backing the development of the Rapid Reaction Force. The

Rapid Reaction Force was an Anglo-French idea, but much of the emphasis must be placed upon the 'Anglo'. Tony Blair has seen this as an opportunity for the European Union to become involved properly in any regional problems. The disaster of Kosovo must not be repeated. The Rapid Reaction Force would also mean less dependence upon the United States.

The problem with the CFSP is that there is still a need for agreement among twenty-five member states. In global terms, the European Union is definitely an economic power. The military capability is nowhere near as impressive. The Rapid Reaction Force will be a very small army of around 60,000 troops. Getting it to do anything will be very difficult, indeed – even with regard to humanitarian aid or peacekeeping. The EU is a civilian power, although some of the individual member states have fairly impressive military muscle.

The development of the single currency

There is sometimes a perception that the formation of the single currency, the euro, was something new. Such ideas had been around for many years, however, including the **Werner Plan** in 1969. Werner, the prime minister of Luxembourg, envisaged a staged development of a single currency by 1980. His plans did not come to fruition.

The idea of European monetary union has been around since the 1970s. The whole idea of monetary union requires a range of factors. The first of these is a single **monetary policy**. In effect, all member states have to agree to the amount of money in circulation and the standardisation of a single interest rate and a single inflation rate. Added to this, there would need to be a single authority – one body to be in charge of setting interest rates, etc. Obviously, this would have to be a central bank. Thirdly, there would need to be a harmonisation of macro-economic policies. This would lead to the full development of a single market. Finally, there would need to be a single currency.

As noted above, the idea of a single currency is not new. The Werner Plan established 'the snake in the tunnel'. This pegged all EEC currencies (the six member states and those involved in the first wave of enlargement) against the US dollar. There was a bracket within which the currencies could fluctuate by $+/-2.25$ per cent. There had been massive speculation against the US dollar in 1971, and the hope was that 'the snake in the tunnel' would protect the European currencies. To protect them still further, there was also to be limited divergence between the strongest and weakest EEC currencies (at $+/-2.25$ per cent). This system was unsuccessful as individual currencies were unable to keep within the parameters and were forced to float freely.

The next attempt was the establishment of the exchange rate mechanism (ERM) as part of the European monetary system (EMS). This was established in 1979. It was hoped that the EMS would create a degree of stability within the EC currencies. A European currency unit (ecu) was established as the focal point of the EMS. All trade between EC partners was carried out in ecus. The idea of the ERM was to create this stability by enabling EC currencies to fluctuate by $+/-2.25$ per cent from an agreed point of parity, which was their value against the ecu. This was very similar to 'the snake in the tunnel' but was not tied to the US dollar. If a currency was unable to keep within its given rate of fluctuation, the banks were expected to intervene. Ultimately, the idea of the ecu was to enable Europeans to come to terms with the concept of a single currency.

In 1989, this whole system was taken a step further with the **Delors Plan**. Jacques Delors, the president of the Commission at this time, pointed out that, of the four basic elements of monetary

---

Box 4.4 The timetable to the single currency

Stage 1 (July 1990 to December 1993)
Free movement of capital in the EC. Closer co-operation on macro-economic affairs.

Stage 2 (January 1994 to December 1998)
Launch a system of central banks to monitor and co-ordinate national monetary policies. Increased supervisory powers for the institutions of the EC/EU. Narrowing of margins of fluctuation within the ERM.

Stage 3 (January 1999 onwards)
Establishment of fixed exchange rates. Granting of full monetary authority to EC/EU institutions. The ecu was converted into the euro (which was launched in January 2002).

union (see above), only one was missing. There was a single market, competition policy and other common economic policies. Only macro-economic policy co-ordination was lacking. Thus, Delors put forward the steps required to achieve the single currency. This was then timetabled within the Treaty of European Union.

The challenge was to get the different currencies and economies of the European Union to converge. To enable this to happen, specific convergence criteria were established. These were detailed in the Treaty of European Union (Article 109j).

The convergence criteria focused on interest rates, inflation rates, currency exchange rates, and the levels of public deficit. Inflation had to be kept to no more than 1.5 per cent above the average of the three member states (who wished to sign up to the single currency) with the lowest rates of inflation. Interest rates had to be kept to no more than 2 per cent above the average of the same three states. The exchange rates had to be kept to within the $+/-2.25$ per cent band, while the public debt of the country had to be less than 60 per cent of national GDP, with the national budget deficit to be no more than 3 per cent of GDP. There were waivers for the last two as they are technically **fiscal policy** not monetary policy.

A European Central Bank (ECB) was effectively operating from June 1998, with the euro being used in tandem with national currencies from 1999. On 1 January 2002, twelve member states began using the euro as their national currency. Britain, Denmark and Sweden had **opted out** (the Danes after an overwhelming referendum voted against adoption).

The British position on the developments towards the single currency has been confused. For example, Margaret Thatcher, as leader of the Opposition, committed Britain to joining the EMS. Upon gaining office, she reneged on the commitment. Britain did eventually join the ERM in the late 1980s, however, only to be unceremoniously kicked out in September 1992 (Black Wednesday). Even during the negotiations on the Treaty of European Union, the British position was one of 'wait and see'. As with the issue around joining the EEC (see chapter 2), the British attitude was one of 'you go on, we'll watch, wait and see'.

Currently it is unlikely that Britain will join the single currency in the near future. Gordon Brown proposed five 'economic tests' that

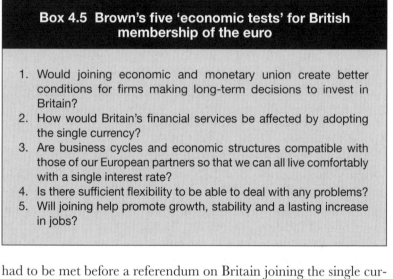

Box 4.5 Brown's five 'economic tests' for British membership of the euro

1. Would joining economic and monetary union create better conditions for firms making long-term decisions to invest in Britain?
2. How would Britain's financial services be affected by adopting the single currency?
3. Are business cycles and economic structures compatible with those of our European partners so that we can all live comfortably with a single interest rate?
4. Is there sufficient flexibility to be able to deal with any problems?
5. Will joining help promote growth, stability and a lasting increase in jobs?

had to be met before a referendum on Britain joining the single currency could go ahead. The tests appear deliberately vague, and may not even be considered 'economic'.

There is a perception in Britain that the euro is not a strong currency. It is true that its value diminished rather rapidly upon formation. Against the US dollar, however, this value has been regained. If anything, the euro is sometimes seen as being stronger than the dollar.

The basic problem with the single currency is that it is difficult to assess its success or failure. European countries have different economic cycles and differing economic problems. These are being harmonised, but it is being done rather more slowly than originally anticipated. There is a feeling that the single currency was a natural step in the process of European economic policy-making. The completion of the single market necessitated a single currency.

The use of the single currency does not have to be seen as a stepping stone to a single Europe. With gradual economic harmonisation, all member states are moving closer together – integrating more. Yet with different languages, cultures, and the strength of national identities, the single currency is not sufficient on its own to lead to a single Europe.

••

✔ What you should have learnt from reading this chapter

- There is a number of different common policies. They have differing aims and objectives, however. Most of them are co-ordinated by the Commission.

- The CAP has been one of the most successful of the common policies. It is in need of reform, however, because of the technological changes that have taken place since the time when the CAP was drawn up. Around half of the EU budget is still spent on agriculture.

- The Common Fisheries Policy is working to preserve fishing stocks while also trying to protect national fishing industries. Some member states, most notably Britain, are unconvinced by the claims of the EU. Half the British (white fish) fishing fleet has been tied up. The other half only operates for half the time. The Common Fisheries Policy is seen as destroying British fishing.

- The Competition Policy and the Common Commercial Policy are working towards protecting EU industry and the rights of the consumer. The EU is very keen to quash anticompetitive practices, and expects any of its trading partners to do the same.

- CFSP is different from the other common policies. It is co-ordinated by the Council of Ministers rather than by the Commission. In some respects CFSP can be seen as a blueprint for a common foreign policy. National interests still override those of the EU.

- Moves to create a single currency for the EU have been around for many years. The Delors Plan, which was timetabled in the Treaty of European Union, led to the formation of the euro. Twelve member states adopted the euro from 1 January 2002.

🔎 Glossary of key terms

Agenda 2000 This is part of the agricultural reforms that were agreed in 1999. It cut the amount of subsidy for farmers in a number of different areas although there were generous compensation packages.

Aquaculture This is the creation or rearing of aquatic (water) life forms.

Common Agricultural Policy (CAP) The CAP was part of the Treaty of Rome although it did not formally come into existence until 1962. The aim was to protect European farming livelihoods while also trying to make Europe self-sufficient in food production.

Common Commercial Policy This common policy focuses on the common external tariff and the quotas of goods that can enter the

European Union. Over time the remit of this policy has been broadened to regulatory issues such as product conformity.

Common Fisheries Policy In 1983, the Common Fisheries Policy came into being. It focuses on preserving fish stocks and the marine ecosystem, as well as on the rights of consumers.

Common Foreign and Security Policy (CFSP) The idea of the CFSP is to encourage co-operation between member states on foreign policy matters. Unlike other common policies, this one is co-ordinated by the Council of Ministers, not the Commission.

Common position This is a step short of a common policy. A common position can be established by the EU but it is very difficult to enforce.

Community preference If there is a choice between an agricultural product from the EU and one from a non-EU state, community preference means that you should buy the community product. To ensure this happens there is a common tariff barrier around the EU to make sure that the non-EU competition is at a higher price.

Competition Policy This policy aims to prevent distortions in competition between private businesses or within the public sector.

Decoupling This was part of the MacSharry plans to reform the CAP. It separated the amount of money paid to farmers from the amount that they produced. It was a move from price support to income support.

Delors Plan The Delors Plan was the timetable to move from EMS and ERM to a single currency for the EU. This plan was timetabled in the Treaty of European Union.

European Agricultural Guidance and Guarantee Fund (EAGGF) This is the scheme which pays out the money for the CAP. The guarantee aspect takes the larger share of the money, focusing on the payments to farmers for their products. The guidance aspect looks at issues to do with farming infrastructure.

European Political Co-operation (EPC) EPC was a precursor to CFSP. It emphasised co-operation between member states in the area of foreign policy.

European Security and Defence Policy (ESDP) This is part of CFSP. The Rapid Reaction Force comes under this policy. It focuses not just on security and defence, but also on humanitarian aid and peacekeeping.

Fiscal policy Government spending.

Monetary policy This looks at the amount of money in circulation, and the ways and means by which it can be controlled, e.g., interest rates.

Opt-out An opt-out can be negotiated by any member state with regard to a policy that may adversely affect national interests. Thus, Britain, Denmark and Sweden opted out of the euro.

Overproduction Quite simply, this is where too much of a product is being supplied. With regard to the CAP, overproduction meant that more food was being produced than was actually required.

Rapid Reaction Force The Rapid Reaction Force is the EU's military response unit. It comes under the CFSP.

Total allowable catch (TAC) TACs are set for each member state. They are national quotas for each type of fish or other from of marine life.

Werner Plan This was the first plan to develop a single currency. It was detailed in 1969/70, and tied all EEC currencies to one another, as well as pegging them against the US dollar.

❓ Likely examination questions

Why has Britain been reluctant to join the single currency? Is it likely that Britain will ever join?

'The Common Agricultural Policy is an outdated piece of legislation. It should be abolished.' Discuss.

'The CFSP is a joke. It is neither common nor does it constitute a common policy. Foreign and security matters tend to be dealt with at the national level.' If this is the case, do we actually need CFSP? Justify your position.

🖥 Helpful websites

www.defra.gov.uk/farm/capreform/pdf/vision-for-cap.pdf is the website for the DEFRA report 'A Vision for the Common Agricultural Policy' published in December 2005.

europa.eu.int/pol/agr/index_en.html gives a comprehensive overview of the activities of the EU within the agricultural sector.

europa.eu.int/pol/cfsp/index_en.html is a web page which covers all aspects of EU foreign policy and security policy.

europa.eu.int/comm/fisheries/doc_et_publ/cfp_en.htm is the Common Fisheries Policy web page. From here you can look at many issues including conservation, facts and figures on fishing stocks and TACs.

europa.eu.int/comm/competition/index_en.html is the homepage for the EU's Competition Policy.

www.europa.eu.int/scadplus/leg/en/s01000.htm is the starting point to examine economic and monetary affairs within the EU. From this website you can move on to the different stages leading to the development of the single currency.

members.tripod.com/~WynGrant/WynGrantCAPpage.html is the home page for Wyn Grant's CAP website.

Suggestions for further reading

L. Cram, D. Dinan, and N. Nugent (eds), *Developments in the European Union* (Palgrave, 1999) has specific chapters on several of the EU's common policies.

A. Deighton, 'The European Security and Defence Policy', *Journal of Common Market Studies*, vol. 40, no. 4 (2002) pp. 719–42.

M. Elsig, *The EU's Common Commercial Policy* (Ashgate, 2002).

R. Fennell, *The Common Agricultural Policy: Continuity and Change* (Clarendon Press, 1997).

W. Grant, *The Common Agricultural Policy* (Macmillan, 1997).

N. Winn, *EU Foreign Policy beyond the Nation-state* (Palgrave, 2001).

CHAPTER 5

The Influence of the European Union on Britain

Contents

Overview

The last two chapters have focused upon the institutions and some of the policies of the European Union. This chapter moves on to how the EU has had an impact upon Britain. The EU has a profound influence upon not just parliament, but also on the regional assemblies in the United Kingdom, and upon local government. In fact, it could be argued that the EU has been a spur to those parts of subnational government that feel distanced – or even ostracised – by central government. Through structural development funds, subnational government has benefited from EU membership – although this point is often missed by most parts of the British media. There is also an important aspect of which we need to be aware, however. This is the changing constitutional relationship between Britain and the EU. The EU has had an impact on the British constitution – and some have argued that this may be irreversible.

Key issues to be covered in this chapter

- The constitutional relationship between Britain and the European Union
- Parliament and the European Union
- The impact of the European Union on regional government in the United Kingdom
- Local government and the European Union

The constitutional relationship between Britain and the European Union

The underpinning of the British system of government is very clear: **parliamentary sovereignty**. In effect, this means that the British parliament is the supreme law-making body in the land. No other institution can challenge the laws of Parliament. Only Parliament can overturn decisions taken by Parliament. It is Parliament that can allocate powers to other institutions such as local government or regional assemblies. Parliament can also take these powers back, however. This means that the British constitution is **unitary** in nature. There is only one source of power: Parliament. In contrast, a federal system of government (as used in Australia, Germany and the United States) dissipates some of the power away from the centre. This dispersion of power is also protected by the constitution.

It has been suggested that the Human Rights Act (1998) challenges the idea of parliamentary sovereignty as it means that the judiciary may be able to challenge Parliament on some of the decisions taken. It is Parliament that granted the judiciary this 'right' (or maybe 'privilege' is a better term), however, and a future Parliament could simply repeal the legislation. There is a similar situation with the legislation enabling devolution. Powers have been granted to the devolved bodies. These powers could be suspended or rescinded – as has been the case with the Northern Ireland Assembly.

Membership of the European Union (or the European Economic Community as it was when Britain joined in 1973) has also provided a challenge to the British constitution. By joining the organisation, the British government accepted that EEC (or EU) law overrides British law when the two conflict. In effect, if there is any legislation in the United Kingdom that runs counter to that of the EU, it must be repealed. Thus, it could be argued, that Britain has surrendered **sovereignty** to the EU in any areas where the EU has the right to legislate. In effect, Parliament is no longer the supreme law-making body in all aspects of British (or more accurately English) law.

While powers have been ceded to the EU, however this does not mean that Britain has lost its sovereignty. All of the laws imposed by the EU can be repealed if Britain was to withdraw from the EU. The British government may have ceded some aspects of law-making to the EU but

Box 5.1 Components of the British Constitution

Statute law Acts of Parliament which override other constitutional sources.

Common law Judicial decisions which establish legal precedents.

Conventions Rules, customs and practices which are considered binding (normally applicable to Parliament).

EU law This takes precedence over national law (where the two conflict).

Law and custom of parliament Guidelines as to how Parliament may operate.

Works of authority Books and writings which are considered as expert guidance on the constitution.

any subsequent Parliament can reverse such a decision. The problem here is that it is rather unlikely that Britain will withdraw from the EU.

The way in which EU membership has been incorporated into the British constitution can be seen by examining the different component parts of the constitution, as shown in Box 5.1. Decisions taken by the EU are still only one aspect of the British constitution. Admittedly, it may be a growing part, but statute law and common law are still prominent as well.

The best-known example of EU law overriding British law was the Factortame case. The British government passed legislation (The Merchant Shipping Act, 1988) to prevent Spanish fishermen 'quota hopping'. This was done by registering their boats as being British and thus landing their catches as part of the British quota of the Common Fisheries Policy. The legislation demanded that all boats on the British register be British owned. This was considered to be discriminatory against Spanish owners and operators, and was against community law. The secretary of state was prevented from enforcing the law.

The European Union and the United Kingdom parliament

Membership of the EU has changed some of the ways in which the British parliament operates. As many directives, decisions and regulations are issued by the EU (which are binding on all member states – see chapter 3 for more details), they still, technically, have to be ratified by Parliament. Thus, there is a number of **select committees** that now exist which scrutinise EU legislation. On average, more than 1,000 documents are scrutinised each year by the House of Commons Select Committee on Europe. As with all select committees, this is a bipartisan or multipartisan body although there is an in-built government majority. This means that all parties with MPs on such a committee work together as opposed to against each other although, if the government so wished, it could force any decisions through the committee. The membership of this select committee is detailed in Box 5.2.

It is not just scrutiny of EU legislation, however, that is performed by the select committee on Europe. It also scrutinises the performance of British ministers in the Council of Ministers. This is on top of the scrutiny that is performed in the House of Commons through such procedures as ministerial (or prime ministerial) question time.

Box 5.2 Membership of the House of Commons Select Committee on Europe (as of January 2006)[1]

Member of Parliament	Party
Jimmy Hood (Chairman)	Labour
Richard Bacon	Conservative
David Borrow	Labour
William Cash	Conservative
Michael Connarty	Labour
Wayne David	Labour
Jim Dobbin	Labour
Michael Gove	Conservative
Nia Griffith	Labour
David Hamilton	Labour
David Heathcote-Amory	Conservative
Sharon Hodgson	Labour
Lindsay Hoyle	Labour
Angus Robertson	Scottish National
Anthony Steen	Conservative
Richard Younger-Ross	Liberal Democrat

The role of keeping ministers in the Council of Ministers accountable for their actions is very important. Arguably, the Council of Ministers, collectively, is not accountable to anybody. Thus, keeping the British ministers accountable is the only form of scrutiny available to the British parliament in an attempt to hold the Council of Ministers accountable for their actions.

Yet it is not only the House of Commons which has a select committee dedicated to the EU. The House of Lords also has a select committee on Europe. It also has seven subcommittees, each dedicated to a particular part of the EU. These are listed in Box 5.3. The formal EU select committee of the House of Lords covers EU documents and other matters pertaining to the EU. The subcommittees are the specialists.

Like the House of Commons, the House of Lords select committees are likely to operate beyond party lines. The House of Lords has a distinct advantage over the Commons, however. There is less party-political pressure within the chamber. This means that the party whips have far less influence. The Lords also tends to be far more thorough with their scrutiny. Much of this is to do with the pressures of time. Members of the House of Lords are able to spend far more time examining legislation from the EU or the actions of British ministers in the Council of Ministers than their House of Commons counterparts.

As well as select committees on Europe, there are also **standing committees**. A standing committee examines legislative proposals between the second and third readings of a bill (see the British

---

Box 5.3 House of Lords committees on Europe[2]

EU Select Committee
EU Economic and Financial Affairs and International Trade
    (Subcommittee A)
EU Internal Market (Subcommittee B)
EU Foreign Affairs, Defence and Development Policy (Subcommittee C)
EU Environment and Agriculture (Subcommittee D)
EU Law and Institutions (Subcommittee E)
EU Home Affairs (Subcommittee F)
EU Social Policy and Consumer Affairs (Subcommittee G)

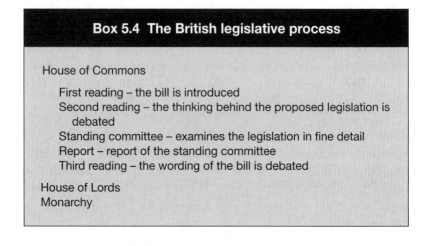

Box 5.4 The British legislative process

House of Commons

First reading – the bill is introduced
Second reading – the thinking behind the proposed legislation is
    debated
Standing committee – examines the legislation in fine detail
Report – report of the standing committee
Third reading – the wording of the bill is debated

House of Lords
Monarchy

legislative process in Box 5.4). A standing committee will examine the legislation in fine detail. As with select committees, standing committees are cross-party (but retain an in-built government majority).

In the past, there were three standing committees to cover EU legislation. This was increased to five in 2005. Of these, three are in existence at the time of writing. The idea of having five such committees is to allow greater specialisation in scrutinising EU legislation.

It is more likely to be the European Select Committee that directs one of the standing committees to examine some legislation. When this happens, any MPs may sit in on the debate and even participate and suggest amendments to the legislation, although they have no voting rights. It is also possible for the debate to be transferred to the floor of the Commons. If it is recommended, there is an obligation for the debate to take place in the standing committee, but no obligation for the government to follow any of the standing committee's recommendations. Failure to do so, however, could lead to problems in the House and, quite possibly, in the media. One way out is often to grant a debate on the floor of the House, particularly if it is a controversial issue.

The European Union and regional government in the United Kingdom

When examining the relationship between the EU and regional government in the UK, it is rather difficult to examine it all as a single block. The Scottish Parliament has significantly greater powers than either the Northern Ireland or Welsh Assemblies. Added to this, regional government in England is wholly unelected outside of the Greater London Authority. As a result, their relationships with the EU may differ. Therefore, it is somewhat easier to examine each region separately. Specific issues with regard to each region will be addressed after highlighting aspects common to them all.

One of the first things to note is that there is regional representation at the EU in the **Committee of Regions**. This body (which was examined in chapter 3) is a purely advisory body. Its recommendations and opinions are not binding. This body, however, does highlight the importance of regional (and local) government representation across the EU. The nominations to the Committee of Regions are co-ordinated at the regional level in Scotland, Wales and Northern Ireland, and by the Office of the Deputy Prime Minister in England. Nominations are sought in consultation with the respective local government associations (from each region). There are twenty-four British delegates, and a further twenty-four alternate members. An alternate member is a substitute if the full member is unable to attend.

Like any other regions throughout the EU, the different regions of the United Kingdom can bid for **structural fund** monies. Over €233 billion worth of funds were available between 2000 and 2006 on the EU-15 (the ten states which joined in 2004 received a separately allocated sum between 2004 and 2006). Of this, Britain received over €18 billion. There are four different funds, but the key one of these is the **European Regional Development Fund (ERDF)**. The others are the Social Fund, the guidance aspect of the EAGGF (see chapter 4), and part of the Common Fisheries Policy.

Regions throughout the EU are categorised with regard to their per capita GDP. Any region with a per capita GDP of less than 75 per cent of the EU average is classified as an Objective 1 region. The next rank is Objective 2. These are regions undergoing social and economic conversion to redress structural problems. Finally, Objective 3 regions are those that require modernisation of their education, training and employment systems and policies. Ultimately, the idea is to increase the economic well-being of every region and to end many of the disparities. Within the EU (pre-2004 enlargement) some regions had unemployment levels of less than 2 per cent (Tyrol, Austria) while others were closer to 30 per cent (Réunion, France). The structural funds are used to redress some of these imbalances.

The regions are also able to bid for monies to improve their infrastructures via the ERDF. Any such bids have to be costed, and the long-term benefits to the region fully explained and evaluated.

Scotland

The devolved government in Scotland has been granted a range of powers. It is able to make **primary legislation** in many areas. This means that the Scottish Parliament may pass laws which differ quite significantly from those in the rest of Britain – including the possibility of varying the rate of income tax by up to 3 pence. In fact, the Scottish Parliament can legislate in any area of policy that is not reserved by Westminster. While foreign matters are one of the reserved areas, this has not stopped the Scottish Parliament from developing its own links with Brussels.

The Scottish Parliament has its own European and External Affairs Committee (EEAC). As with the committees in the Westminster Parliament, the Scottish version monitors the implementation of EU legislation. It also scrutinises the Scottish Executive to make sure that it is being open and transparent about the way in which it implements EU legislation, or the way in which it examines EU issues.

The EEAC has also taken this role much further. For example, an inquiry was set up to examine the 'Transposition and Implementation of European Directives in Scotland'. The aims were to compare the ways in which EU directives were being implemented in Scotland – in specific fields such as agriculture, fishing and the environment – with the implementation processes in England and Wales, as well as other regions of the EU which were of a similar autonomous nature as Scotland. The report is expected to be published in late 2006. The fact that such an inquiry has been established highlights the extent to which Scottish needs and interests are diversifying from those of the rest of Britain.

As well as the Scottish Parliament working on EU relations, the Scottish Executive is also doing the same. The Scottish Executive has developed two divisions on Europe. The first is based in Edinburgh, the second in Brussels. The Edinburgh division, like the EEAC, focuses on how EU directives are implemented in Scotland. It has developed close links with the EEAC. The Brussels division works closely with UKREP (see chapter 3 for more information on this body) in trying to promote and protect Scottish interests in Brussels. The Scottish Executive has even produced a document examining how Scotland can improve its relations with the EU – not just the public sector, but also the private sector. The document is entitled *European Union: Forward Look for 2006* (January 2006).

Wales

The devolved government in Wales has significantly less powers than that of Scotland. Whereas the Scottish Parliament has primary legislative powers, those wielded by the Welsh Assembly enable it to pass only **secondary legislation**. In effect, this means that the Welsh Assembly can only adapt laws already passed by Westminster.

Despite the rather restricted powers of the Welsh Assembly, this has not stopped it from developing links with Brussels. The Welsh Assembly has set up an office in Brussels. This body, which contains European policy specialists, works closely with UKREP. The overarching objective of this office is to promote and protect Welsh interests across the EU.

In Cardiff, there is a European and External Relations Division which is part of the Department of Economic Development and Transport of the Welsh government. This division performs a similar role to that of its Scottish equivalent. These include examining how directives and regulations passed by the EU are best implemented in Wales. This division also examines a range of other issues, however, including preparing for the possibility of Britain signing up to the euro, how this would affect Wales, and how Welsh institutions should be readied for such a changeover (should it ever happen). This is quite a far-reaching scheme but wholly within the devolved remit for Wales.

There is also a European and External Affairs Committee which meets nine times a year. All the meetings are open to the public. The role of this committee is 'to ensure that the National Assembly takes a coherent strategic approach in relation to Europe'.[3] This is done through a range of different methods, drawing in all the different bodies with which the Welsh Assembly interacts. Yet again, there are the ideas of promoting Wales and protecting Welsh interests.

Northern Ireland

Though the devolved bodies in Northern Ireland are not sitting (at time of writing), the relationship between them and the European Union is still documented very clearly. In working out what committees were required for scrutinising the Northern Ireland Executive, it was acknowledged that a committee of some sort would be needed to scrutinise EU legislation as well.

An EU affairs subcommittee was established. This is one of thirteen subcommittees of the Committee of the Centre. The role of the Committee of the Centre is to scrutinise the work of the First Minister and Deputy First Minister, as well as other matters decided by the Northern Ireland Assembly.

It is interesting to note that, while the Northern Ireland Assembly felt it important to scrutinise all directives from the EU, it acknowledged that it could not influence them once they had been made. The British parliament could veto them but that would be a nuclear option – such an option was not available to the devolved assembly.

From the position of the executive of Northern Ireland, the specific department that focuses on the EU is the Department of Enterprise, Trade and Investment (DETI). Although the assembly and the executive are not currently sitting, DETI is still working towards getting more inward investment into Northern Ireland. The EU is one of the primary channels. An EU Programme for Peace and Reconciliation in Northern Ireland ran from 2000 to 2004. It was a joint Ireland/Northern Ireland programme and was more commonly known as the Peace II programme. A previous programme of Peace and Reconciliation had run from 1995 to 1999. The five main priorities of Peace II, which were funded through the EU structural funds, were:

- economic renewal;
- social integration, inclusion and reconciliation;
- locally based regeneration and development strategies;
- outward and forward looking region;
- cross-border co-operation.[4]

The total amount of money to be spent between the years 2000 and 2006 was around €531,000,000, split 80 per cent – 20 per cent between Northern Ireland and the border regions of the Republic of Ireland.

London

With the Greater London Authority (GLA) and the London Mayor, there is a twintrack representation for Londoners. The Mayor of London (Ken Livingston) has a European Policy Agenda. This focuses upon the development of London, and how the EU has an impact here. It also looks at how London can have an impact upon the rest of the EU.

There is also a London Plan. This aims to reinvigorate public services in London. It is being modelled upon EU guidelines in areas such as spatial development.

In Brussels, there is a London European Office. This was opened in November 2001. Like all the equivalents from the other devolved bodies, this office looks to represent the interests of London in Brussels. Another aim of this body, however is to promote and utilise London expertise in areas such as housing for the rest of the EU. The London European Office sees a strong reciprocal relationship between itself (as the representative of London in Brussels) and the institutions of the EU.

A final point to note about London is that it is, if anything, overrepresented on the Committee of Regions. Currently, five of the twenty-four British delegates are there to represent London. Compared to any other region across Britain, there is a far greater weight behind the concerns of London than anywhere else. It could be argued that this is because London is the capital city. No other capital city in the EU has such overrepresentation, however.

England (outside London)

The problem with regional government in England (outside London) is that it is unelected. There are **regional development agencies**. These are listed in Box 5.5. The powers of each agency are the same. Their remit was specified most clearly in the legislation that led to their creation.

Box 5.5 Regional development agencies in England

Advantage West Midlands
East Midlands Development Agency
East of England Development Agency
London Development Agency
North West Development Agency
One North East
South East England Development Agency
South West of England Regional Development Agency
Yorkshire Forward

The regional development agencies (RDAs) – which were set up in April 1999 – were originally envisaged to be a stepping stone towards elected regional government in England. This has not happened. One referendum has been held on such a move (in the north-east of England). Any move towards elected regional government was defeated overwhelmingly. This leaves the RDAs operating under the same remit as when they were first created – that of the economic regeneration of their region as well as improving the skills and competitiveness. The terms of reference are the same for each RDA.

Although different strategies may adopted by the different RDAs, it is easier to focus upon one of them to get a picture of how the EU is having an impact upon the regions of England. The East Midlands Development Agency (emda) has set itself the target of getting into the top twenty EU regions of where people want to live and work by 2010. Issues such as jobs, income, regional GDP, environmental matters, and equality are included among the statistics that are taken into account when measuring the regions. Since its inception, emda has moved from thirty-fifth to twenty-eighth, and, with more EU funding being injected into the region, the aim of becoming a top-twenty region is achievable. The next review of funding in 2006, however, is likely to see a reduction in funds for emda (and all English RDAs) as structural funding is likely to be redirected to many of the regions of the new East European member states.

Emda works with various private organisations, as well as with subregional bodies, to encourage EU investment into the East

Midlands. In fact, emda has also established an East Midlands European Office (EMEO) in Brussels as part of a strategy to promote the region in the EU. EMEO also represents the concerns of local government bodies in the East Midlands as well as those of the RDA. Emda is very keen to highlight the importance of working with the various EU institutions, as well as being a conduit for information to be directed to those other bodies which would benefit from contact with the EU. This is one of the reasons why emda claims to be the leading RDA in England when it comes to relations with the EU.

Local government and the European Union

During the 1980s and 1990s, local government across Britain saw its powers being reduced by central government – part of the Thatcherite ideal of 'rolling back the frontiers of the state'. Through access to the EU (or EC as it then was), however, local authorities were able to access new monies (over and above the central block grant) to develop infrastructure or to create new employment opportunities. These monies came from the various structural funds – particularly the Regional Development Fund and the Social Fund.

Today, local authorities work with the EU (often alongside other tiers of government) in aspects of service delivery as well as policy formulation. The most notable point of access in the policy formulation process is via the Committee of Regions. As noted earlier in this chapter (as well as in chapter 3), the Committee of Regions gives regional and local government input into the policy-making processes of the EU. This enables all tiers of government to have the opportunity for input into EU decisions. Currently, of the United Kingdom's twenty-four members of the Committee of Regions, eighteen are local government representatives from across Britain.

What is interesting about the relationship between local government in Britain and the EU is that there has been a marked development in collaboration. This collaboration is not only between British local government and the EU but also between the different tiers of local government – particularly on a regional basis – to further their collective interests. As with the RDAs, the East Midlands will be used as a case study.

As noted earlier in this chapter, the East Midlands European Office (EMEO) has a key role in promoting the region. This is done through a partnership between, among others, emda and all of the local authorities in the East Midlands. The EMEO has helped to develop an integrated strategy to capture funds for the region. This is only possible through the hard work done at a local, as well as a regional, level.

The local authorities themselves are also very active with regard to the EU. For example, Leicester City Council has a European Office within its Regeneration and Culture Department. This office works to secure EU funding for the city, quite often alongside EMEO and emda, as well as other local authorities. As Leicester has Objective 2 status for Social Fund monies (see earlier in this chapter for an explanation), a considerable amount of EU funding is directed into the city. The city council is the body which is accountable for how that money is spent.

Conclusion

What can be seen from this chapter is that all parts of government across Britain have access to the EU and potential funding from the EU. The constitutional relationship between Britain and the EU may be a little blurred at times but membership has had a huge impact upon how the different tiers of government across Britain operate. It has been **subnational government** that has taken up the baton in developing more positive links with the EU. This can be seen at every tier of subnational government. Central government seems to have a less close relationship with the EU. Much of this could be to do with money. Britain is a net contributor to the EU budget – thus, central government loses money. The various tiers of subnational government are able to access funds from the EU, over and above what they receive from central government. This extra funding can then be targeted at specific regional or local needs. It makes for a rather complex relationship – to the extent that perhaps we should not look broadly at EU–UK relations but should look more closely at the relationships between the EU and the different tiers of government in Britain.

● ●

✓ What you should have learnt from reading this chapter

- The underpinning of the British constitution is parliamentary sovereignty. This has not been undermined by membership of the EU. No British government can bind its successors. Therefore any future British government could legislate to withdraw from the EU.

- British central government has a number of different committees to scrutinise EU legislation as well as the actions of the British government within the Council of Ministers. There are committees from both chambers of Parliament. The select committees are particularly influential, as they are able to call ministers and civil servants to explain their actions.

- At the regional level, elected and unelected governments have opened up offices in Brussels. From these, the different regions of Britain are able to promote their own interests as well as attempting to influence policy-making.

- The Committee of Regions is the body which tries to promote and defend local and regional interests of the EU. Although it is only an advisory body, there is a compulsion for its opinions to be sought in specific policy areas.

- Local government in Britain has benefited from extra funding from the EU through the structural funds. These are monies in addition to that received from central government.

🔎 Glossary of key terms

Committee of Regions This is an advisory body created under the Treaty of European Union. Delegates are selected from regional and local government from each member state. Any policy proposals that affect regional or local government must be put before the Committee of Regions.

European Regional Development Fund (ERDF) This is one of the structural funds. The ERDF focuses upon developing and improving the infrastructure of regions across the EU.

Parliamentary sovereignty This is the underpinning of the British constitution. In effect, Parliament is the supreme law-making body in Britain. There is no judicial review of parliamentary legislation. No other body can legislate against Parliament – to do so would be to act ultra vires (beyond the law). Only Parliament can repeal legislation made by previous parliaments. Thus Parliament cannot bind its successors.

Primary legislation In Britain, if an institution is given primary legislative powers, this means that it can pass any legislation that is not reserved for

Westminster. Bearing in mind the idea of parliamentary sovereignty, however, such primary legislative powers can be returned to Westminster.

Regional development agencies (RDAs) These quangos were established in 1999, originally as a stepping stone to creating directly elected regional governments in England. The RDAs have a clear remit to stimulate the economic regeneration of their respective regions. They are given a budget by central government but are also able to generate other sources of revenue as well, e.g., accessing EU structural funds.

Secondary legislation This is where the broad outline of a law is passed by Parliament but it is then fine tuned by another tier of government to suit its particular needs.

Select committee In Britain's parliamentary system, select committees were established as an extra form of scrutiny of the executive. Members on these committees can call for any person or paper to be brought before them. Even members of the public could be asked to come before a select committee, as a result of their expertise in a given area, or even to explain some of their actions.

Sovereignty This is the right to make laws over a given territory. A state is sovereign in that it has this right. There is also external sovereignty, however, where a state would have to be recognised by other states as being sovereign. Such recognition legitimises a regime.

Standing committee Within the legislative process of the British Parliament, a standing committee convenes after the second reading of a bill. The committee works through the proposed legislation in fine detail, trying to find ways of improving the legislation. There is one handicap here – the government has an inbuilt majority on a standing committee. It is possible that this majority could be used to prevent any amendments to the legislative proposals.

Structural funds These funds are used by the EU to develop regional policy. In particular, the structural funds are used to narrow some of the disparities between the richest and poorest regions of the EU. There are four specific aspects: the European Regional Development Fund (ERDF); the European Social Fund; the European Agricultural Guidance and Guarantee Fund (EAGGF); and part of the Common Fisheries Policy.

Subnational government The various tiers of government below national (or central) government. This can comprise regional and local government (of which there may also be multiple tiers). Subnational government is not necessarily elected.

Unitary constitution A constitution allocates power and responsibilities. It is sometimes referred to as 'the rules of the political game'. A unitary constitution means that there is only one source of constitutional power. In the case of the United Kingdom, this is Parliament. There are also federal constitutions, where power may be dispersed from the centre. This dispersal of power is normally protected by the constitution, and is very difficult to change.

? Likely examination questions

'Parliamentary sovereignty has been compromised by EU membership. Britain is no longer a sovereign state.' Discuss.

Membership of the EU has had a profound impact upon the structures of government across Britain. Yet the reality is that this is a reciprocal relationship. In what ways have the different tiers of British government had an impact on the operation and policy-making of the EU?

The EU appears to be targeting regional and local government in an attempt to bypass central government. Assess the benefits of such an approach. Do we need to retain central/national government?

Helpful websites

www.parliament.gov.uk/documents/upload/TheEuroScrutinyCommitteeint heHoC.pdf is a guide for MPs on the role of the European Scrutiny Select Committee.

www.scotland.gov.uk/Resource/Doc/923/0021839.pdf is the web address for *European Union: Forward Look for 2006*, which is a document produced by the EU Office of the Scottish Executive.

www.scottish.parliament.uk is the home page of the Scottish Parliament. This is a starting point to see all the different aspects of the Scottish Parliament that are influenced by the EU.

www.scotland.gov.uk is the home page of the Scottish Executive.

www.wales.gov.uk is the website for the Welsh Assembly. From here it is also possible to find out about the executive of the Welsh Assembly.

www.niassembly.gov.uk is the home page of the Northern Ireland Assembly. At the time of writing, the Assembly was not sitting.

www.london.gov.uk is a starting point to find out about the government of London. From here, it is possible to go to the London Assembly web pages or those of the London Mayor. It is also a starting point to find out how the EU and London interact.

www.englandsrdas.com/home is the home page for all of the regional development agencies in England. From here you can access your own RDA, or any other. For the best access to information on the EU, try the East Midlands Development Agency at www.emda.org.uk.

Suggestions for further reading

I. Bache, 'Multi-level Governance and European Union Regional Policy' in I. Bache and M. Flinders (eds), *Multi-level Governance* (Oxford University Press, 2004) pp. 165–78.

S. Bulmer, M. Birch, C. Carter, P. Hogwood and A. Scott, *British Devolution and European Policymaking* (Palgrave, 2002).

B. Dickson, *The Legal System of Northern Ireland* (SLS, 2001).

S. George, 'Multi-level Governance and the EU' in I. Bache and M. Flinders (eds), *Multi-level Governance* (Oxford University Press, 2004) pp. 107–26.

M. Keating, *The Government of Scotland* (Edinburgh University Press, 2005).

M. Smith, 'Britain, Europe and the World' in P. Dunleavy, R. Heffernan, P. Cowley and C. Hay (eds), *Developments in British Politics 8* (Palgrave, 2006) pp. 159–73.

CHAPTER 6

Intergovernmentalism versus Supranationalism

Contents

Overview

Having examined the structures and the policies of the European Union, it is now important to set them inside a theoretical context. The EU is pulled in different directions. This chapter will focus on the debate between intergovernmentalism and supranationalism. The future development of the EU is linked to these two approaches. Some of the EU institutions are seen as being intergovernmental, while others are perceived to be more supranational in character. There is a clear conflict between these two approaches – they may be seen as contradictory and even irreconcilable. Despite this conflict, the EU seems to function more than just adequately. From a British perspective, the debate between these two approaches is very important. An organisation that is seen as being supranational may be viewed as a threat to national sovereignty. Such a threat does not exist to the same degree, if at all, in an intergovernmental organisation.

Key issues to be covered in this chapter

- Definition of the concept 'supranationalism'
- Definition of the concept 'intergovernmentalism'
- How these two approaches affect the institutions and the policies of the EU
- The impact of these two approaches on British membership of the EU

What is supranationalism?

To detractors of the EU, the concept of 'supranationalism' carries much emotional baggage. **Supranationalism** means loss of national sovereignty, greater **integration**, and ultimately the formation of a United States of Europe. The EU, as a supranational organisation, is to be questioned, resisted, and perhaps even ostracised. Nations must resist this idea.

The problem is that such emotive language actually distorts the idea of supranationalism. In the long term, there may eventually be an ultimate move to form a United States of Europe, but a supranational approach does not necessarily guarantee that such a union will occur.

So what is supranationalism? This is where some states have ceded some decision-making powers to a higher authority – in this case, the EU. These decision-making powers are only in specified areas, such as agriculture, however, and thus the Common Agricultural Policy. It is important to note that, although these decision-making powers have been ceded to the EU, they can be returned to the individual states. So, although critics may see this ceding of decision-making powers as a ceding of **sovereignty** to the EU, the reality is that a state can withdraw from the organisation at any time.

Part of the perceived problem with supranationalism is that the authority to which powers are ceded is independent of the member states. Its decisions are binding on all member states – in fact, they override national law should the two conflict. Such a situation highlights the fact that supranationalism is far greater than mere co-operation between countries. In specified areas, the higher authority is the supreme decision-making body.

The effects of supranationalism go much further than this, however. Linked to the idea of supranationalism is that of **spillover**. This concept can be seen to focus upon the consequences of supranationalism – the knock-on effects of the decisions being taken. In some respects this can be seen as being related to Adam Smith's idea of 'the invisible hand'. Smith's idea was that the consequences of a specific decision that has been taken benefit everyone. Yet these consequences were not intended by the decision-makers. Had the decision-makers tried to achieve such an outcome, it is most likely that they would have failed to achieve their original target. Thus, there was an invisible hand influencing the outcome. Smith attributed such outcomes to God.

With regard to supranationalism and the EU, movements in specific policy areas have unintended outcomes in others. For example, decisions taken in the environmental sector may have unseen consequences for agriculture (or vice versa). The creation of the single market has had an impact on employment law in all member states. In each case, the spillover helps to speed up the process of EU integration.

Supranationalism and the European Union

Within the EU there are supranational institutions – although not all of the institutions are supranational in nature. It could actually be argued that no body is totally supranational or, for that matter, intergovernmental but rather that they are all a combination of the two.

The institution that is most associated with the concept of supranationalism is the Commission. There is full coverage of this institution in chapter 3, but it is useful to reiterate some of the supranational aspects of the Commission here. The first thing to note about the Commission is that, although there is one commissioner from each member state (which appears to be intergovernmental), all commissioners take an oath of loyalty to the Commission. Thus, although Peter Mandelson is Britain's commissioner, he is first and foremost the Trade Commissioner for the EU. The same applies for each commissioner with regard to their relationship with their state and their portfolio.

One of the aims of the Commission is to promote greater integration within the EU. The concept of integration is examined in chapter 7. In brief, it is about getting the member states to work together more and more closely. By doing this, there is a greater need for co-ordination at the supranational level to ensure that there is consistency in policy-implementation across all EU member states. This co-ordinating role has been taken on by the Commission. In doing so, the Commission is in a position to make policy proposals (for consideration by the other institutions of the EU). This leaves it clearly in the role of a supranational policy-maker.

Other bodies that could be seen as at least partly supranational include the Court of Justice (as well as the Court of First Instance) and the European Parliament. Like the Commission, the members of both courts are selected from each member state. Once on either court, however, the members are expected to put the position of the EU ahead of any national interest. Decisions taken by the courts may affect the entire EU, not necessarily just one member state.

The European Parliament is the only directly elected body in the EU. As a parliament, you might expect the members to have a mandate from the European people to make laws on their behalf. This is not the case. As can be seen in the example in Table 6.1, the members sit in ideological transnational groupings (like-minded thinkers from different member states). The problem is that the actual elections are all held at the national level, on different days and using different electoral systems. Thus, within each ideological grouping of the European Parliament, there is a wide range of opinions which are covered. For example, the British Conservative and Unionist Party is not very enthusiastic about working towards 'ever closer union', although many other members of the Group of the European People's Party do not share that opinion. In this case, however, the divisions are becoming so wide that it has been suggested that the British Conservative Party will withdraw from the Group of the European People's Party after the next elections to the European Parliament in 2009.

As can be seen in Table 6.1, it could be argued that, by bringing so many disparate parts of the EU together, the European Parliament actually performs a supranational role. Thus, in many respects, each political grouping within the Parliament actually has to function like any other national political party (except it is EU-wide) in trying to draw together a wide range of political perspectives under one umbrella. In doing this, there is a hope that proper trans-European political parties will start to develop across the EU.

Supranationalism and the United Kingdom – a troubled relationship?

Within British politics, the idea of supranationalism is equated with the development of a European superstate. Much of the British

Table 6.1 Breakdown of an ideological transnational grouping of the European Parliament

Group of the European People's Party and European Democrats (January 2006)[1]

Alleanza Popolare – Unione Democratici per l'Europa (Italy)

Centre Démocrate Humaniste (Belgium)

Christen Democratisch Appèl (Netherlands)

Christen-Democratisch & Vlaams – Nieuw-Vlaamse Alliantie (Belgium)

Christlich Demokratische Union Deutschlands (Germany)

Christlich Soziale Partei (Belgium)

Christlich-Soziale Union in Bayern e.V. (Germany)

Coligaçao Força Portugal (Portugal)

Conservative and Unionist Party (UK)

Det Konservative Folkepartei (Denmark)

Dimokratikos Synagermos (Cyprus)

Erakond Isamaaliit (Pro Patria Union) (Estonia)

Evropští demokraté (Czech)

Fidesz-Magyar Polgári Szövetség (Hungary)

Fine Gael Party (Ireland)

Forza Italia (Italy)

Gia tin Evropi (Cyprus)

Jaunais laiks (Latvia)

Kansallinen Kokoomus (Finland)

Křesťanská a demokratická unie – Československá strana lidová (Czech)

Kresťanskodemokratické hnutie (Slovakia)

Kristdemokraterna (Sweden)

Table 6.1 (continued)

Group of the European People's Party and European Democrats (January 2006)[1]

Magyar Demokrata Fórum (Hungary)

Moderata Samlinspartiet (Sweden)

Nea Dimokratia (Greece)

Nova Slovenija (Slovenia)

Občanská democratická strana (Czech)

Österreichische Volkspartei – Liste Ursula Stenzel (Austria)

Parti chrétien social (Luxembourg)

Partido Popular (Spain)

Partit Nazzjonalista (Malta)

Partito Pensionati (Italy)

Platforma Obywatelska (Poland)

Polskie Stronnictwo Ludowe (Poland)

Slovenská demokratická a krest'anská únia (Slovakia)

Slovenska demokratska stranka (Slovenia)

SNK sdruženi nezávislých a Evropští demokraté (Czech)

Strana mad'arskej koalíicie – Magyar Koalíció Pórtja (Slovakia)

Südtiroler Volkspartei (Partito popolare sudtirolese) (Italy)

Tautas partija (Latvia)

Tèvynès sajunga (Lithuania)

Ulster Unionist Party (UK)

Unión del Pueblo Navarro (Spain)

Union pour un Mouvement Populaire (France)

Unione dei Democratici cristiani e dei Democratici di Centro (Italy) media can be particularly vitriolic when it comes to any aspect of supranationalism. Unsurprisingly, much of this opinion within the British media is ill-informed. It can be boiled down to a pseudo-patriotic, anti-foreigner bias. Anything that comes from Europe must be bad – and if it is not, then it is not mentioned.

Whenever powers are ceded to the European Union, the focus is upon the loss of British sovereignty. The EU is portrayed as faceless bureaucrats in Brussels taking over British lives and telling everyone what to do – to use grams and kilograms rather than pounds and ounces; to use centimetres and metres rather than inches and yards. Soon it will be kilometres rather than miles, and we will have to drive on the right hand side of the road! In the television series *Yes, Minister*, the Minister for Administrative Affairs, Jim Hacker, in an anti-European outburst, talks of the British being compelled to eat salami and bratwurst rather than traditional British sausages. When she was Prime Minister, Margaret Thatcher commented that Britain had surrendered enough sovereignty. In a speech to the College of Europe in Bruges in the late 1980s, Thatcher spoke of the creation of identikit Europeans. The suggestion was that, as the member states moved closer and closer together, they would lose their national identities.

This apparent fear in Britain of supranationalism is rather difficult to source. There is some conjecture that it stems from our being an island nation – but that falls apart somewhat when the attitudes towards supranationalism in the Republic of Ireland are taken into account. Ireland is even further away from the rest of Europe but has a far more positive outlook on supranationalism. An alternative perspective is the idea that Britain is an 'old' state. History books tell us that Britain has not been invaded since 1066. All other European states are relatively new. Most of Europe had to be reconstructed economically and politically after World War II. Britain did not suffer any of the political reconstruction. Thus, 'surrendering' sovereignty and national identity to a supranational organisation comes somewhat more easily to those on the Continent.

Yet all this might be more of an 'English' thing. The Scots and the Welsh seem far more enthusiastic about the EU. The Scottish Nationalist Party (SNP) has conducted general election campaigns under the slogan 'An Independent Scotland within Europe'. It may well be that many people in Scotland and Wales see Britain being run for the benefit of England – and possibly even London. Consequently, they are exploited. Within British politics, for example, the poll tax was introduced into Scotland as an experiment a year before it was introduced into the rest of the United Kingdom. There are also many stories of economic exploitation of the Scots (North Sea oil and gas) and the Welsh (coal and steel industries) by the English. To prevent such perceived abuse from the dominant partner within the United Kingdom, Scotland and Wales look more and more to Europe (see chapter 5 for more information). Therefore, to the Scots and the Welsh, supranationalism at the European level may be little different from that at the UK level.

What is intergovernmentalism?

If the concept of supranationalism carries with it much baggage, the same cannot be said of **intergovernmentalism**. Quite simply, intergovernmentalism is about different national governments working together. There are many different intergovernmental organisations around the world, including the United Nations, NATO, the World Trade Organisation (WTO) and ASEAN (Association of South East Asian Nations). The emphasis is very much upon the individual state or government. Whereas the concept of supranationalism includes ceding of sovereignty to a higher authority, there is no such commitment with intergovernmentalism. The individual states remain sovereign. They are the supreme decision-making bodies.

In the post-war years, many intergovernmental organisations were established. The most prominent were the defence pacts around the world – the two most obvious being NATO and the Warsaw Pact. In the case of NATO, there was no compunction to remain a member. Thus, France was able to withdraw. Such freedom for manoeuvre was not so available for those under Soviet domination – although Albania did withdraw from the Warsaw Pact in the late 1960s.

Economic trading blocs have also been established. Again, these are intergovernmental organisations. There is no ceding of sovereignty to a supranational centre. Examples of such trading blocs include CER (Closer Economic Relations [between New Zealand and Australia]) and EFTA (European Free Trade Association (see chapter 2).

Intergovernmentalism and the European Union

There is an unresolved debate in the European Union as to whether it is a supranational organisation or an intergovernmental one. As has been noted earlier in this chapter, there are aspects of the EU which are supranational. There are also aspects of the organisation which are clearly intergovernmental.

The Council of Ministers and the European Council (both of which are examined in chapter 3) are the most obvious examples of intergovernmental institutions within the EU. While the Council of Ministers is still seen as the most important institution within the EU, the reality is that its role is far more about protecting national interest than furthering the aims and objectives of the collective body. Even disputes, in the early years of the organisation, such as the Luxembourg Compromise (see chapter 2), highlighted the extent to which national interests were prioritised. The idea that any country could veto any legislative proposals if they were not in their national interest demonstrated that, despite any degree of integration, national self-interest would predominate. While there may be some 'surrendering of sovereignty' within the EU, no national government is going to legislate for its own demise.

As the name suggests, intergovernmental conferences are little more than a gathering of the member states to hammer out any differences before trying to agree a common position. It is even possible for states to agree opt-outs, for example, at the Maastricht Summit, Britain opting out of the Social Charter, and both Britain and Denmark opting out of the single currency.

Looking at the Treaty of European Union, one term in particular highlights the extent to which the EU is an intergovernmental body: **subsidiarity**. This concept was promoted by the then British prime minister, John Major. The idea of subsidiarity is to devolve decision-making away from the centre to the most appropriate level of government. For Major, this meant taking decision-making powers away from the EU/Brussels and handing them back to national governments. Admittedly, some member states, and this now includes Britain, saw subsidiarity as also devolving decision-making away from national governments to regional or local tiers of government. Regardless of which interpretation of subsidiarity is used, both show that the EU is quite clearly an intergovernmental organisation.

The European Council, where the different heads of government meet, is often seen as the symbol of intergovernmentalism. This is where the different national prime ministers and presidents get together. While some may see this as the symbol of national co-operation under the banner of the EU, at the end of the day it is still the heads of the different governments working together.

A prominent symbol of the EU as an intergovernmental body is the presidency of the Council of Ministers. As noted in chapter 3, this is on a six-monthly rotation, with each member state getting its turn. When holding the presidency, each member state is in a position to push its national agenda for the EU. Thus, when Britain held the presidency in the second half of 2005, reform of the CAP and the budget, as well as enlargement to include Turkish membership of the EU, were the key priorities. When Austria took over in 2006, the priorities changed.

All the EU institutions have an intergovernmental aspect. The European commissioners are selected from each member state; MEPs are elected in elections held within each member state; members of the Court of Justice, the Court of First Instance, the Committee of Regions and the Economic and Social Committee are all selected at a national level. While there may be some EU input into these various selection processes, the fact is there is always going to be a national element retained. If this were to be dropped then some member states might feel that their national inputs were not necessary. This could lead to withdrawal from the EU. For example, although the commissioners are all national nominations, the European Parliament only has the power to sack all of the Commission. It cannot target a particular individual as that would be likely to harm national sensibilities. Thus, the intergovernmental aspects appear to override those of a supranational slant.

Intergovernmentalism and the United Kingdom

Within British politics, the idea of the EU as a predominantly inter-governmental organisation sits far more comfortably than regarding it as a supranational one. In this way, the British government is able to portray itself as protecting British interests within the EU. Sovereignty is protected, and the British Parliament remains supreme. There are times when Britain does not get its own way in the EU – but the same applies to all member states. If there appears to be a threat to national interest, however, any member state can attempt to veto the policy proposals. Thus, in the negotiations on the Treaty of European Union, the British position on the single currency was to opt out, but not to block such a move. There was a similar position with the Social Charter. Any plans to make the European Parliament into a legislative body, however, were blocked with the threat to veto the entire treaty. This was one of the British **red lines**; it was non-negotiable.

The intergovernmental aspects of the EU mean that the British government has to negotiate with other governments to get legislative proposals accepted (or blocked, when it is not in the national interest). Thus, intergovernmentalism is often about negotiation and compromise, of 'pressing the flesh' as ministers or the prime minister visit their counterparts in other EU states. Tony Blair has been particularly good at this. He has developed a close rapport with many of the new member states, such as Poland. Such intergovernmental alliances can be fickle. In the negotiations to reform the CAP in 2005 (under the British presidency of the EU), when it was suggested that all the new member states get less money in return for Britain giving up part of its budgetary rebate, Blair was suddenly isolated from almost all members of the EU.

Conclusion

In sum, the EU represents a mix of supranationalism and intergovernmentalism. The different institutions carry examples of each, as has been noted above. The supranational aspects of the EU appear to be working towards greater integration – a subject which is examined in the next chapter. Where intergovernmentalism dominates, the emphasis is far more upon the interests of the individual member state.

From a British perspective, the supranational institutions and common policies of the EU are sometimes portrayed as being a threat to British sovereignty. An intergovernmental approach sees a greater emphasis placed upon protecting British interests. Different British prime ministers have come back from intergovernmental conferences and treaty negotiations proudly proclaiming to have got the best possible deal for Britain. The benefits for the collective EU are underplayed – they may even seem inconsequential to the national media, especially parts of the print media that sometimes appear almost europhobic in nature.

··

✅ What you should have learnt from reading this chapter

- The differences between supranationalism and intergovernmentalism are quite clear cut. Supranationalism sees some aspects of sovereignty ceded to a higher body. Intergovernmentalism focuses upon the different governments working together (while protecting their national interests) without ceding any sovereignty.

- Some institutions of the European Union are supranational in nature, for example, the Commission. Others, such as the Council of Ministers are intergovernmental. All EU institutions have a mix of supranationalism and intergovernmentalism.

- Britain appears to be very wary of any aspects of supranationalism. This is often portrayed as 'surrendering' sovereignty. Many people are far more comfortable with the intergovernmental aspects of EU membership – the idea of the British government working with others but ultimately protecting British interests. Much of the British print media is virulently opposed to almost any aspect of EU supranationalism.

🔎 Glossary of key terms

Integration The idea here is of combining a range of different pieces into a single body. Within the context of the EU, this is where the different member states move closer and closer together, and may eventually become one.

Intergovernmentalism This is the idea of the different governments of the EU working together. There is no ceding of sovereignty to a higher body. Each member state remains sovereign and may well work to protect its national interests. An intergovernmental approach would see the different member states working together to achieve some form of compromise.

Red line In any form of negotiations there are red lines. These are the points which are non-negotiable. There will be no compromise over them. If this cannot be achieved then the negotiations will be vetoed.

Sovereignty This is the right of a state to pass laws within its own territory. It is suggested that EU membership undermines national sovereignty as all members have to cede a range of powers to the EU. Added to this, EU law overrides national law when the two conflict.

Spillover The idea of spillover is a possible consequence of supranationalism. A policy that is implemented in one area may have unseen consequences in another. Thus, agricultural policy, for example, spills over into environmental policy. Spillover also helps to speed up the integration process.

Subsidiarity This is the idea of devolving decision-making down to the most appropriate level. In the context of the EU, this meant taking some of the decision-making powers away from the EU/Brussels and returning them to the national governments. These powers could be devolved further to regional or even local government, depending upon which tier was the most appropriate.

Supranationalism Such an approach sees countries working closely together. They cede sovereignty in certain areas to a higher authority which will co-ordinate and police the making and implementation of policies in those specified areas across the organisation.

? Likely examination questions

Why does the idea of supranationalism cause so much concern across the United Kingdom?

Evaluate the extent to which 'spillover' actually occurs within the European Union.

'The European Union is an intergovernmental organisation. Any supposed ceding of sovereignty is merely a sop to supranationalists and those working for a United States of Europe.' Discuss.

Helpful websites

The website www.brugesgroup.com will give you some interesting material highlighting negative aspects of EU membership, that is, opposition to supranationalism. The Bruges Group is not overly enthusiastic about all aspects of the EU although the website does provide a range of both pro- and anti-EU links.

Another website with a somewhat more balanced approach is The European Foundation at www.europeanfoundation.org.

The UK branch of the Commission has some interesting material at www.cec.org.uk. One article in particular focuses on Europe Day at www.cec.org.uk/whatsnew/may9.htm and draws this into supranationalism.

Suggestions for further reading

J. Colomer, 'The European Union: Federalism in the Making' in J. Colomer (ed.), *Political Institutions in Europe* (Routledge, 2002) 2nd edition, pp. 279–307.

C. Jensen, 'Neo-functionalism' in M. Cini (ed.), *European Union Politics* (Oxford University Press, 2003) pp. 80–92.

CHAPTER 7

Expansion versus Integration

Contents

Overview

The whole debate of expansion versus integration is often reduced to that of a wider EU (that is, more members) versus a deeper EU (that is, greater integration; more supranationalism). This is often presented as a 'zero sum' game. It is a choice of one or the other. To attempt to achieve both is not seen as being feasible although it could be argued that the EU is, indeed, trying to do both. As the EU member states develop an integration programme, it does become more difficult for other countries to join. Yet there is a position which says that twenty-five member states is already too many and that such a large membership is slowing down the integration programme. There may be moves at some time in the future towards developing a two-speed Europe. On the one hand, there will be those who desire greater integration, and on the other, those who do not.

Key issues to be covered in this chapter

- Definition of integration
- How is the European Union developing a programme of integration?
- The position of Britain on greater integration
- Definition of expansion
- How can the European Union expand further?
- The British position on further expansion

What is integration?

Many commentators talk about **integration** without necessarily defining the term. It is often associated with the idea of 'deepening' an organisation. This 'deepening' could be of policies or of institutions. Without doubt, the idea of integration can be linked to **supranationalism** (a term which was examined in the previous chapter).

Integration can be seen as a process of bringing disparate parts together and uniting them into a single body. Once this body is operating, the different parts can be pulled closer and closer together, that is, greater integration. The more this integration process continues, the more difficult it will become for any individual member to be able to withdraw. Each member becomes tied in to the organisation. This process of integration can be via common institutions or common policies. It is a form of uniting a group of actors to work for a common goal. This goal could be economic, political, military, and so on.

Different organisations can have differing degrees of integration. The EU is seen as the most highly integrated of all international organisations. Other organisations, with lesser degrees of integration, include: NATO which is a defence pact between a number of European and North American countries; CER (Closer Economic Relations) which is an economic and trade agreement between Australia and New Zealand; and ASEAN (Association of South East Asian Nations) which is an economic and political pact between a number of nations in South-east Asia.

How is the European Union promoting integration?

The integration of member states has always been an important aspect of the European Union. The issue has always been over the extent of the integration, that is, how deep? Arguably, the ultimate end in the integration process will be a United States of Europe – although it is not really a short-term, or even a medium-term, strategy.

Any prospective member state is expected to sign up to the *acquis communautaire*. The *acquis communautaire* comprises all the prior legislation that has been passed by the member states. Any country which wishes to join the EU has to pass this entire legislative package. In doing so, the prospective member state is integrating into the pre-existing structures and is also accepting all the prior legislation that has already been passed. There are no 'opt-outs' available for the *acquis communautaire*. There was an *acquis communautaire* of sorts, even when Britain joined in 1973. With the last enlargement in May 2004, however, it had grown into a package of several thousand pieces of legislation.

In the 2004 enlargement negotiations, the *acquis communautaire* was divided into thirty-one separate chapters, each of which had to be accepted by the applicant states. These chapters are detailed in Box 7.1. As can be seen in the box, the various chapters are quite extensive, covering all aspects of political, economic and social life. They comprise a comprehensive package of often complex legislation.

Looking at the history and development of the EU, the idea of integration has always been in the background. The original European Coal and Steel Community required a degree of integra-tion from the founder members for it to be a success. As governments, businesses and the trade unions saw the benefits of this organisation, plans were made for similar projects in other sectors. This was how **spillover** (see chapter 6) was intended to happen. Successful integra-tion in one aspect of the economy would lead on to other sectors trying to do the same. Thus, an integrated agricultural policy required some-thing similar in transport and the environment for it to be fully inte-grated. The end result would be a fully integrated economy.

Such an ideal seemed to falter in the 1970s. There was talk of the integration programme foundering. Some cynics have attributed this to Britain joining the EEC, but the problems went far deeper. There were serious economic and social problems across the community but there appeared to be no European leadership in addressing them. Instead, each of the member states went its own way. Radical lead-ership was needed to rejuvenate the membership – some sort of con-certed pan-European programme. Instead, the EC appeared to sit back and wait for something to happen.

The integration programme was given something of a kick start with the Single European Act (SEA) and the Treaty of European Union (TEU). These looked at ways in which the idea of greater European integration could be taken forward. Not only was there the

---

Box 7.1 The chapters of the *acquis communautaire* for the 2004 enlargement

Chapter 1: Free movement of goods
Chapter 2: Freedom of movement for persons
Chapter 3: Freedom to provide services
Chapter 4: Free movement of capital
Chapter 5: Company law
Chapter 6: Competition policy
Chapter 7: Agriculture
Chapter 8: Fisheries
Chapter 9: Transport policy
Chapter 10: Taxation
Chapter 11: Economic and monetary union
Chapter 12: Statistics
Chapter 13: Social policy and employment
Chapter 14: Energy
Chapter 15: Industrial policy
Chapter 16: Small- and medium-sized enterprises
Chapter 17: Science and research
Chapter 18: Education and training
Chapter 19: Telecommunications and information technologies
Chapter 20: Culture and audio-visual policy
Chapter 21: Regional policy and co-ordination of structural instruments
Chapter 22: Environment
Chapter 23: Consumers and health protection
Chapter 24: Co-operation in the fields of justice and home affairs
Chapter 25: Customs union
Chapter 26: External relations
Chapter 27: Common foreign and security policy
Chapter 28: Financial control
Chapter 29: Financial and budgetary provisions
Chapter 30: Institutions
Chapter 31: Other

---

idea of the single market, but also a social agenda was pushed forward, with schemes such as the Social Charter. The introduction of the single currency has been seen as one of the largest steps in the integration processes. Although not all member states have signed up to the euro, all those who joined in 2004 (and any other future members) are expected to work towards joining the single currency – chapter 11 of the *acquis communautaire* covers this point (as noted in Box 7.1). It is unlikely that all the new member states will join the euro in the near future but there is an expectation, if not a requirement, that they will join eventually. Slovenia is expected to be the first of the 2004 enlargement states to adopt the euro in 2007.

While the SEA and the TEU gave a clear kick-start to the integration process, it may have stalled again with the failure to adopt the EU constitution. This document, in effect, codified much of the legislation that the EU had already passed. In many cases, the constitution simplified what already existed. Failure to get the constitution ratified in France and the Netherlands, however – where referendums were defeated – and members such as the United Kingdom and Poland no longer attempting to ratify the constitution, mean that the integration process has stalled again.

Where the idea of integration has taken great steps forward is through the concept of **governance**. This is where the different tiers of government can feed into one another. The different inputs can come to (or from) the various tiers of government – local, regional, national or European. They interact with one another. Some decision-making processes such as an agriculture, have moved to the centre while others have moved in the opposite direction through the concept of **subsidiarity**.

Yet this idea of governance should not be restricted solely to the roles of the different tiers of government. It means far more. Across the European Union, no longer is it seen that 'government' must be the sole provider of goods and services. Rather, there can be a range of providers, and not all of them from the public sector. With bodies such as the Economic and Social Committee (ESC) (see chapter 4), special interests get an input into the decision-making process. Admittedly, the ESC is only an advisory body but it has expert opinion which can be useful not only in policy formulation but also in implementation. Thus, we see a new form of integration as the different sectors work together.

It is not only at one tier of government that we see this occurring. There is multi-level governance – across the different tiers of government (as noted above) – as well as non-governmental organisations also being drawn into the processes. Thus, in Britain private companies can be involved in service delivery at the local level. For example, Biffa (formerly part of Severn Trent Water) empty the refuse bins in Leicester. Prior to Biffa winning this contract, it was a French company (SITA) who provided the service. Bids, or tenders, are put in for these types of services. Guidelines are issued to give advice on what is required in the service provision. The local authorities examine the tenders, looking for the best value for money and quality of service.

In many respects, multi-level governance can be seen as the epitome of the integrationist ideals. Not only are the different tiers of government working together, but so are the different sectors – private, public and voluntary. Such integration was probably beyond the expectations of many of the founders of the European ideal.

Yet there is still the question of how much further integration is needed or is necessary? It could even be summed up as: 'what is the end goal of integration?' To these questions there is no clear and definitive answer. Some Euro-enthusiasts might argue that the ultimate goal is a United States of Europe: a single country with one federal government and beneath that a number of 'state' governments, not dissimilar to that which exists in the United States of America. Arguably, this could be the end result if the integration process continues. The different member states tie themselves closer and closer together under the EU institutions.

Such an end result is unlikely to happen because of the extent of intergovernmentalism (see chapter 6) within the EU. Many member states – most notably Britain – are protective of their national sovereignty. The idea of greater integration will be resisted. Some proposals could even be vetoed if the threats to national sovereignty were perceived to be too great.

The United Kingdom and integration

The apparent position of all British governments on the issue of integration has been one of reluctance. The idea of the 'reluctant European' will be examined in chapters 8 and 10. On the issue of integration, however, Britain's reluctance appears to come to the fore. As noted earlier in this chapter, much of the debate around the idea of greater integration is very similar to that of supranationalism. The British position on supranationalism was covered in chapter 6. There are, however, a few key points that need coverage with regard to integration.

Most British governments – and especially those under Thatcher and Major – were seen as being concerned over the process of integration. It was associated with the idea of surrendering sovereignty. Yet there were aspects of the process of integration where these and other administrations have actually been enthusiastic. One such example concerns the development of the single market. The idea of having free trade across all member states, with no tariffs or duties, has appealed to governments of all natures. Such a set-up ties in all the member states economically – their economies integrate more easily under a single market. It was over political integration that there were (and still are) stumbling blocks. This is where the idea of 'surrendering sovereignty' appears.

With political integration, the result is a supranational set up. As the member states of the European Union integrate politically, it is the EU structures that take over many aspects of policy-formulation. This is particularly important when bearing in mind the constitutional position – that EU law overrides national law when the two conflict. Thus, most British governments have been rather reluctant to support aspects of political integration (and sometimes economic integration). Major, for example, negotiated opt-outs from the single currency and the Social Charter. Such ideas were seen as going too far down the integration line and were to be resisted. Britain was quite happy, however, for the other member states to proceed. There was no attempt to stop the integration of other members if that was what they wished to do.

One result of the British lack of enthusiasm over integration has been the talk of a **two-speed Europe**. The idea here is that those member states that wish to pursue greater integration should be allowed to do so. Those that do not should not be compelled to do so. Yet there is a surprising lack of support in Britain for such an approach. One reason for this can be linked back to spillover. As the part of Europe which desires deeper integration goes ahead with such plans, the consequences of their actions and policies would be likely to draw the less enthusiastic members down the integrationist path. An alternative could be the exact opposite. A two-speed Europe could lead to the fragmentation of the European Union into two autonomous organisations – one that has integrated; the other being a loose collection of states. Neither approach is particularly appealing to the British government, nor to any other member state for that matter. Thus, whenever there is talk of a two-speed Europe, it is never greeted with much enthusiasm.

One way of fighting the idea of greater integration, which has been utilised by British governments, is support for increased membership of the European Union. With a larger number of members, it is more difficult to go down the integrationist line. This could be one reason why Britain has been particularly supportive of proposed Turkish membership of the EU. A wider trading bloc, with only limited political integration, seems to appeal to many in the British government. The integration process can be slowed down, and is then easier to sell to the British people.

Where British governments have been more enthusiastic over integration is through the concept of governance. In many respects, it is Britain that has been leading the way in drawing in private-sector organisations into public-sector service delivery. The idea in Britain is that private-sector organisations are more effective and more efficient than those in the public sector. Yet what has been used in Britain is a combination of both. Britain has been trying to sell this approach to the rest of the EU. There has been considerable reluctance from some members – most notably France and Germany. The new members from Eastern Europe are far more enthusiastic about the British approach to governance. They also wish to encourage the use of private-sector organisations in service delivery. This is likely to lead to even greater economic integration and further strengthen ties within the single market. As a result, the regulatory powers of the EU will need to be increased. Consequently, there will be a degree of spillover into increased political integration – something that the British government would be rather unenthusiastic about.

The expansion of the European Union – what are the limits?

The debate about the expansion of the European Union – or, more accurately, EU enlargement – is often seen as an opposite to integration. The more member states that are in the EU, the more difficult it becomes to increase the degree of integration. Yet the debate about widening the EU is still important in its own right. How big can the EU become? What states could join?

There have been four stages of enlargement to date, with a fifth due in 2007. Each of these earlier enlargements has already been examined in chapter 2. The fifth enlargement, to include Bulgaria and Romania, can be seen as a continuation of the 2004 enlargement. In 2004, eight former communist, East European countries joined the EU (along with Cyprus and Malta). Bulgaria and Romania were not permitted to join at that stage because they were unable to comply with the Copenhagen Criteria (see earlier in this chapter). It is widely anticipated, however, that they will meet the requirements for enlargement to take place in 2007. Thereafter, the issue becomes slightly more problematical.

Currently, several countries have expressed an interest in joining the EU. Those whose applications are being considered are Turkey and Croatia. Other countries have also expressed an interest in joining. These include Bosnia, Serbia and the Ukraine. Added to this, Armenia and Georgia have also expressed interest in future membership. Finally, Morocco and Algeria have raised the possibility of application as well. Such interest from all of these countries raises the question of the limits of the EU. Where can the final boundaries be drawn?

A final point to note about any future enlargements is that such decisions are taken by unanimous voting. All member states must support an application for it to go ahead. Thus, as more countries join the EU, it will get more difficult to achieve unanimity.

Turkey
There has been a number of Turkish applications to join the European Union. Until recently, they have all been vetoed. The EU outlined to Turkey, however, a number of issues that would need to be addressed for Turkish membership to be considered. Most of these are encapsulated in the Copenhagen Criteria. On top of this, specific mention has been made of human rights issues, and the extent to which Turkey has become an open, liberal and secular state. A final question over Turkish membership has been whether or not Turkey is even part of Europe. For many commentators, the Bosporus Straits

from the boundary between Europe and Asia. Most of Turkey is situated on the Asian side. Thus, Turkey should not be considered as part of Europe. It has even been suggested that, if Turkey joins the EU, then its neighbours may also be eligible. This includes Syria and Iraq!

Yet such a debate on geography is a little disingenuous. Turkish history is linked with Europe. In fact, at one time, the Ottoman Empire stretched as far as Vienna. Developments in the Balkans, both past and present, have been influenced hugely by Turkey.

What is of greater concern to some members of the EU is that Turkey is an Islamic country. There is a fear that, by allowing Turkey into the EU, it may enable the spread of Muslim fundamentalism across Europe. Such scaremongering ignores the point that there are already millions of Muslims living across Europe, while the 'fundamentalist' label is used to suggest possible terrorist activity.

Ultimately, the Turkish application will hinge on their achieving the Copenhagen Criteria. The economic underdevelopment of Turkey is such that this is not likely to happen in the near future. Membership is being pencilled in for 2014, but a lot can happen between now and then. One of Turkey's biggest supporters in the EU, Britain, has argued that such a timescale gives Turkey time to develop and modernise its economy, as well as to improve its human rights record.

Western Balkans

This grouping covers the countries that used to comprise Yugoslavia: Croatia, Bosnia, Serbia, and the former Yugoslav republic of Macedonia; along with Albania. All these countries are at different stages along the EU application process. Croatia is the furthest advanced, Albania the least. All the former Yugoslav republics have similar issues to address. Much of this stems from events during the war in Bosnia in the early 1990s. There are alleged war criminals in each country, and potential EU membership is conditional upon them being surrendered to The Hague to stand trial for these crimes at the International War Crimes Tribunal.

Steps have been taken to encourage all of these countries to join in the peaceful rebuilding of the region. The 'carrot' of encouragement is possible EU membership. Much of this was detailed at the

Thessaloniki Summit in June 2003. It included areas such as human rights, economic reform and regional co-operation, and it all goes on top of the Copenhagen Criteria.

Like Turkey, Croatia is looking to EU membership in 2014. The Croats have some interesting sponsors in the EU, most notably Austria. The Austrians were apparently able to get the Croats into the application process as a *quid pro quo* for not vetoing the Turkish application in 2005 (during the British presidency of the EU).

Both Bosnia and Serbia see their futures within the EU. For the Bosnians, membership of the EU would enable the rebuilding of the country to continue apace. Serbia's desire to join can be linked to a need to rebuild civilised contact with the rest of Europe, particularly after the problems during the Milosovich regime. There are still fundamental issues such as the future of Kosovo which need to be addressed, however.

The Thessaloniki Summit has instilled the whole Western Balkans region with both hope and expectation. The development of the region is going to be a long, slow process, particularly noting the economic underdevelopment. Croatian inclusion in the EU will be a spur to the other countries in the region.

Former Soviet republics

It is not just in the Western Balkans that there are countries with aspirations to join the EU. Some former Soviet republics have seen the Baltic states (Estonia, Latvia and Lithuania) join the EU and this has sparked greater enthusiasm for EU membership. The Ukraine is to the forefront in pushing for membership. But it is not alone. Countries such as Armenia, Azerbaijan and Georgia have also expressed interest. It must be noted, however, that Russia has made it known that these countries all come under its sphere of influence, and that potential EU membership would put a great strain on Russo–EU relations. This has not stopped the EU from developing trade-and-aid links with Armenia, Azerbaijan and Georgia.

The EU position is that these countries are part of a wider Europe and should not be excluded from the benefits of such a Europe. This comes under the **European Neighbourhood Policy (ENP)**. The ENP is all about helping the political, economic and social development of countries that have little chance of EU membership in the near future.[1] It also includes countries that are not geographically part of Europe (for example, North Africa, see below). For the likes of Armenia, Azerbaijan and Georgia, there is a carrot – albeit a distant one – of potential EU membership.

North Africa and the Middle East

A number of countries have expressed interest in joining the EU despite not being part of Europe. North African countries, particularly Morocco and Algeria, have expressed an interest in joining the EU – in fact a Moroccan application for membership was rejected in 1987. The rejection was on the grounds that Morocco was not a European country. Instead, these countries have a preferential trading status via the Euro-Med partnership, as do countries such as Egypt, Jordan, Lebanon, the Palestinian Authority and Syria. The EU-MED12 agreement was signed in 1995 – although two of these countries have since joined the EU (Malta and Cyprus) and another (Turkey) has entered into negotiations for membership. The agreement covered a number of areas including trade and regional security. These southern Mediterranean countries are also included in the ENP (see above) although it is unlikely that an offer of EU membership will be extended to them. Any future developments, however, may hinge on Turkey joining the EU, and the development of EU relations with Armenia, Azerbaijan and Georgia. Morocco, in particular, is awaiting the result of the Turkish application. Should Turkey be successful, it is most likely that Morocco will reapply for membership, despite the geographical reasons for exclusion in 1987.

The United Kingdom and enlargement

The United Kingdom is probably the most enthusiastic supporter of increasing the membership of the European Union. In fact, enlarging the EU seems to have been something of a priority. Cynics could argue that this is little more than a subtle plan to stop greater integration. The more members there are in the organisation, the more difficult it becomes to deepen the Union.

The British position is quite clearly not to let just any country join. The Copenhagen Criteria form a key part of the British position on enlargement. Applicant states must meet these criteria and accept the *acquis communautaire* to be allowed to join the EU. Thus the Turkish application, of which Britain appears to be a sponsor, could easily stall if its human rights record is not improved markedly. Similarly, any of the West Balkan countries that wish to join the EU will have to comply in full with the demands of sending all indicted war criminals to The Hague for trial. Failure to do so will be a bar to EU membership.

British support for enlargement can be seen as part of a larger game plan. With more countries joining, and with the vast majority likely to be net beneficiaries from the EU budget, this will give the opportunity for Britain to argue for a reform of the Common Agricultural Policy (CAP) as well as the budget as a whole. Many of the pre-2004 members of the EU, which were net beneficiaries from the budget, are likely to see that position change with each subsequent enlargement. The various structural funds are likely to be redirected to the less well-off regions of Eastern Europe. Members that are net contributors to the budget are likely to see their contributions increase! Thus, vested interests will see reform of the budget and the CAP before there are any future enlargements of the EU. This is very much a long term strategy.

Where Britain may have a problem over subsequent enlargements concerns the eventual boundaries of the EU. There is an argument that Europe stretches from the Atlantic to the Ural Mountains in Russia, and from the Arctic Ocean to the Mediterranean Sea. This would include countries such as Norway and Switzerland (who do not want to join the EU) but could be seen to exclude Armenia, Azerbaijan and Georgia (who do wish to join), and possibly even Turkey. The possible membership of Turkey could enable Armenia and Georgia to join as they border Turkey. Azerbaijan would probably be included as a 'group package'. Added to this are other former-Soviet states such as Moldova and Belarus, which are geographically part of Europe. Arguably, Britain would like to see the opportunity of membership extended to all of these countries, subject to their achieving the Copenhagen Criteria.

The possible drawback of such an increased membership would be that Britain's voice in Europe would be further diluted. Although one of the 'Big Four' member states, with each enlargement, Britain's voice in the EU is diminished. An EU with between thirty and forty member states would potentially see any one individual state as little more than a bit player in the region. This would apply as much to Britain as to France or Germany. Any future enlargements will also see the epicentre of Europe move further and further east. From a British perspective, this may not be a good thing as the demands of northern and western Europe are significantly different from those in the south and east.

The inclusion of Bulgaria and Romania is expected in 2007, however. The next applicant countries (Croatia and Turkey) are not likely to join until 2014. Any subsequent enlargements are in the distant future.

•••

✅ What you should have learnt from reading this chapter

- The idea of integration means bringing together a range of bodies and gradually uniting them. It is sometimes described as 'deepening' an organisation.

- The European Union promotes integration via the development of common policies such as Agriculture or Foreign and Security Policy

- Britain is often seen as rather reluctant about greater EU integration. It is often perceived as leading to further loss of sovereignty.

- Enlarging the EU is about increasing the membership of the organisation. There are strict requirements (Copenhagen Criteria) which have to be met before a country can join the EU.

- Britain is quite keen to have further enlargement of the EU, subject to the meeting of the Copenhagen Criteria. There is a suspicion that British enthusiasm for enlargement may be in part to prevent greater integration.

🔎 Glossary of key terms

Acquis communautaire This is the package of treaties and legislation which has already been passed by the EU that any new member states must accept as part of joining the European Union.

European Neighbourhood Policy (ENP) The ENP focuses upon helping countries which are geographically close to Europe, and enabling them to benefit from the EU. Owing to their lack of economic (and political and social) development, these countries are unlikely to be able to join the EU in the near future.

Governance At one level, governance is about the different tiers of government feeding into one another. Yet it can also include non-governmental bodies, such as private businesses or voluntary organisations. All these have a stake in policy formulation and implementation.

Integration The idea here is one of combining a range of different pieces into a single body. Within the context of the EU, this is where the different member states move closer and closer together, and may eventually become one.

Spillover Spillover is a possible consequence of supranationalism. A policy that is implemented in one area may have unseen consequences in another. Thus, agricultural policy, for example, spills over into environmental policy. Spillover also helps to speed up the integration process.

Subsidiarity This is the idea of devolving decision-making down to the most appropriate level. In the context of the EU, this meant taking some of the decision-making powers away from the EU/Brussels and returning them to the national governments. These powers could be devolved further to regional or even local government, depending upon which tier was the most appropriate.

Supranationalism Such an approach sees countries working closely together. They cede sovereignty in certain areas to a higher authority which will co-ordinate and police the making and implementation of policies in those specified areas across the organisation.

Two-speed Europe This approach is where different parts of the EU integrate at different rates. There would be a fast track of deeper integration and a slow track of more gradual integration. Arguably, there could be a multispeed Europe.

Likely examination questions

'The European Union's integration programme has the ultimate aim of creating a United States of Europe.' Discuss.

'Any further enlargement of the European Union beyond that proposed for 2007 is likely to lead to the demise of the EU.' Evaluate this perspective.

Greater integration will diminish Britain's voice in the EU. Further enlargements will do the same. Evaluate possible courses of action for future British governments.

Helpful websites

For information on EU integration, it is easiest to examine the material by subject area. The europa index is the best place to start, at www.europa.eu.int/index_en.htm

www.europa.eu.int/pol/enlarge/index_en.htm is the EU web page on enlargement. There is comment here about the 2004 enlargement as well as the Thessaloniki Summit and the future membership of Croatia. There is also another EU web page (under development at the time of writing) at www.europa.eu.int/comm/enlargement

The Foreign and Commonwealth Office home page at www.fco.gov.uk is a useful starting point on Britain's position on enlargement. Go to the Britain and Europe section, and then on to enlargement.

Suggestions for further reading

L. Cram, 'Integration Theory and the Study of the European Policy Process' in J. Richardson (ed.), *EU Power and Policymaking* (Routledge, 2001) 2nd edition, pp. 51–73.

M. Cremona (ed.), *The Enlargement of the European Union* (Oxford University Press, 2003).

S. Mazey, 'European Integration: Unfinished Journey or Journey without End?' in J. Richardson (ed.), *EU Power and Policymaking* (Routledge, 2001) 2nd edition, pp. 27–50.

C. Preston, *Enlargement and Integration in the EU* (Routledge, 1997).

H. Sjursen, 'Why Expand? The Question of Legitimacy and Justification in the EU's Enlargement Policy', *Journal of Common Market Studies*, vol. 40, no. 3 (2002) pp. 491–514.

S. White, I. McAllister and M. Light, 'Enlargement and the New Outsiders', *Journal of Common Market Studies*, vol. 40, no. 1 (2002) pp. 135–53.

CHAPTER 8

Political Parties and the European Union

Contents

Overview

The attitudes of the different political parties in the United Kingdom to the European Union can be described as problematic. A key reason for this is that no party is unified on this subject. While there may be clear guidance on the position of the party leadership, this is not necessarily followed by all members or representatives of the party. If anything, the European Union is one subject that cuts across party lines. It has resulted in situations that have been described as 'unholy alliances' across the British political parties – both in support of, and in opposition to, further developments in the Union. On top of this, as the European Union has developed, the major parties have changed their positions on it. In some cases, they have moved from opposition to membership to support of membership and vice versa. The same also applies to some of the minor parties.

Key issues to be covered in this chapter

- An historical overview of the positions of the major British political parties on the EU
- An assessment of the extent to which the positions of the major parties may have changed over time
- An evaluation of the current positions of the parties on the EU
- How some of the smaller parties stand on the issue of the EU

Conservative Party

The Conservative Party has traditionally been seen as the flag-waving, patriotic, pro-British political party. It has also been seen as a more pro-European party than its nearest rival, the Labour Party – although both originally opposed entry into either the European Coal and Steel Community or the European Economic Community. In fact, it was a Conservative government that first applied to join the then EEC in 1961, and it was a Conservative government that took Britain into the EEC in 1973. Even during the early 1980s, when Margaret Thatcher was demanding 'our money back', the Conservative Party was still considered to be the party of Europe. Much of this could be attributed to the anti-European stance of the Labour Party at that time. Yet, in the elections to the European Parliament in 1979 and in 1984, it was the Conservative Party that gained most of the British seats.

Such a perspective glosses over an important point, however. This is that the Conservative Party has not been united over Europe. There was dissent among the party ranks – even in the 1961 application, with the likes of Enoch Powell speaking out strongly against EEC membership. In 1971, two junior ministers, Teddy Taylor and Jasper More, resigned over the EEC application of the Edward Heath government. The cabinet, if not the rest of the party, appears to have been unanimous in supporting the application. Even getting the legislation through the Commons required the support of the Labour Party, as can be seen in Box 8.1. Thus, taking Britain into the EEC was not easy for the Conservative Government of the day.

As can be seen in Box 8.1, there were divisions in both the major parties. The first reading of the European Communities Bill was designated a **free vote** by the Conservative Party, although the Labour Party attempted to enforce a **three-line whip**. All subsequent votes were whipped.

Since the passing of the legislation to take Britain into the EEC, the Conservative Party has appeared to be broadly pro-European. Even though there were the endless demands for the return of British money during the Thatcher years, Thatcher saw Britain's role as being inside the European Community. In that way, she would be able to protect British interests far more effectively. British interests would

Box 8.1 Vote on EEC membership in the House of Commons (1971–2)

First reading (free vote) 28 October 1971	Yes	No	Abstain
Conservative and Ulster Unionist	282	39	2
Labour	69	198	20
Liberal	5	1	–
Others	–	6	–
	356	244	22

Government majority 112

Second reading (three-line whip) 17 February 1972			
Conservative and Ulster Unionist	304	15	6
Labour	–	279	5
Liberal	5	1	–
Others	–	6	–
	309	301	11

Government majority 8

Third reading (three-line whip) 13 July 1972			
Conservative and Ulster Unionist	295	16	*
Labour	–	263	*
Liberal	5	–	1
Others	1	5	–
	301	284	*

Government majority 17

* number unknown

override those of the EC. In this respect, Thatcher was sometimes described as a **Tory Gaullist** in that she followed the stance of the former French President, Charles de Gaulle, who put national interests ahead of those of Europe. Thus, Thatcher's attitude to Europe was not so much the problem, but rather it was her modus operandi that seemed to cause a stir.

In the latter years of her premiership, Thatcher seemed to become a little removed from mainstream thinking within her party. She highlighted fears of the creation of 'identikit Europeans' in a speech in Bruges in 1988. Ultimately, it seemed that Europe had moved on and Thatcher was left behind.

The problem has been that the Thatcherite legacy has left the Conservative Party rather directionless on the issue of Europe. All her successors have had huge problems in trying to unite the party over the issue of Europe. John Major was able to pilot the Treaty of European Union through the House of Commons using brinkmanship. He effectively said to Conservative MPs who were opposed to the treaty that they had two choices: accept what he had negotiated, with the opt-outs for the single currency and the social charter; or oppose what he had negotiated, lose a subsequent general election, and have a Labour government accept the treaty without all of the opt-outs. Major even withdrew the party whip from eight Conservative MPs over the issue of Europe. They were joined by a ninth, Sir Richard Body (MP for Holland with Boston). The removal of the party whip from these MPs technically left Major with a **minority government**! Major also had problems within his Cabinet over the issue of Europe. In an unguarded moment, he spoke into a microphone, which he believed to be turned off, of the 'cabinet bastards' – referring to the right-wing Eurosceptic members of his Cabinet. It was generally believed that he was referring to Michael Howard, Peter Lilley and Michael Portillo.

Ultimately, the divisions over Europe within the Conservative Party have split the party. Today, there are still MPs such as Andrew Rosindell (MP for Romford), who would like to see Britain withdraw from the EU. He approves of a European free-trade area but believes that the European Parliament should be abolished. Yet there are also members of the Conservative Party who have highlighted the importance of Britain signing up to the euro – most notably, the former

Chancellor Kenneth Clarke. The more enthusiastic members of the EU within the Conservative Party are a distinct minority.

William Hague and Michael Howard led the party – though it could be argued that the party took both of them – down a more Eurosceptic route. William Hague's 2001 General Election campaign focused upon 'saving the pound'. Such an approach had appeared successful in the 1999 elections to the European Parliament, where the Conservatives became the largest British party. With a turnout of only 24 per cent, however, too much may have been read into how convinced the British public actually was on this issue. In the 2001 General Election, the more Hague pushed 'saving the pound', the more steadily support moved away from the party. It was only when he focused on other issues that support returned to the Conservatives. Michael Howard was somewhat cannier over Europe, highlighting negative aspects of the proposed European constitution. Yet neither he nor Hague gave serious consideration to realigning the Conservative Party within the European Parliament. Despite their often apparently anti-EU rhetoric, the Conservative Party stayed with the grouping of the European People's Party (EPP). This grouping is broadly in favour of greater integration in the European Union, something that most Conservative MEPs do not support. Yet staying in the EPP gives the Conservatives far more influence.

The latest leader of the Conservative Party, David Cameron, has been described as the most Eurosceptic leader of the Conservative Party. Within weeks of winning the party leadership, he mooted the idea of leaving the EPP (see Table 6.1 for the full membership of the EPP). He is not actually able to do this until 2009, so it will be interesting to see how the Conservatives will realign themselves within the European Parliament after the next elections. It has been pointed out that one alternative would be to align themselves with Silvio Berlusconi's Forza Italia Party. This is not really seen as a viable option as Forza Italia contains an eclectic range of individuals, some of whom are alleged to have associations with the Italian neo-fascists. There have also been suggestions that the Conservatives might realign with a Polish anti-European party but, as this party also wants to outlaw abortions, it is unlikely that the Conservatives will go with them.

The current position of the mainstream Conservative Party appears to be reluctant acceptance of EU membership. Renegotiation of EU membership, and even possible withdrawal, have been mooted, however. The feeling in some quarters of the Conservative Party is that Britain would do far better outside the EU, having negotiated a free-trade agreement, without suffering all the burdens of regulation from the Union. There is a belief that the EU needs Britain more than the other way around. At the time of writing, David Cameron appears to accept that Britain is in the EU but that any further integration is a non-starter. The majority of the Conservative Party seems to support this position although the numbers arguing for withdrawal seem to be on the increase.

Labour Party

While the Conservative Party has always seemed broadly to accept membership of the European Union and its predecessors, the same cannot be said of the Labour Party. Thatcher may have earned the label 'reluctant European' because of her attitude towards Europe, but the Labour Party is just as deserving of the label. It has switched between support of membership and opposition to membership on more than one occasion. Even within the Labour Party, there are probably more divisions on the issue of Europe than in the Conservative Party.

Labour originally opposed membership of the European Coal and Steel Community. It also refused to support Harold Macmillan's application to join the EEC in 1961. Its first U-turn was to apply for membership in 1967 – although it must be noted that not all of the party supported this application.

In the 1970 General Election, the Labour Party campaigned to 'negotiate terms of entry'. The wording meant that even those who were less than enthusiastic about possible EEC membership could be placated under such a slogan. Added to this, it meant that the Labour Party was not committed to joining the EEC. An agreement on possible terms of entry might not be reached.

As can be seen in Box 8.1, the Labour Party was divided on whether or not to support the Conservative government on entry into the EEC. Deputy Party Leader Roy Jenkins led sixty-eight other Labour MPs into the 'Aye' lobby, defying a three-line whip in the process. During the legislative process, and after the legislation was passed, the official Labour Party position was to contest the deal that

Heath's government had negotiated. Harold Wilson committed the Labour Party to renegotiating the terms of entry and then to put them to a national referendum. This proposal forced Roy Jenkins into resigning from the Labour Party deputy leadership.

After winning both the 1974 general elections, Harold Wilson suspended **collectivity** over the issue of Europe. This meant that any members of the Cabinet could campaign either for or against membership. Once the referendum was over, however, all members had to accept the outcome. It was an astute move by Wilson, as the Labour Cabinet was deeply divided on EEC membership. Tony Benn was stridently against membership, as was Peter Shore. Barbara Castle, on the other hand, was far more enthusiastic about Europe. In the referendum campaign, Benn was willing to share a platform with Enoch Powell in his campaign against membership. With the referendum returning a convincing 'Yes' vote, it seemed that divisions over EEC membership subsided within the Labour Party – publicly, at least.

All this changed after the 1979 election defeat. Michael Foot was elected Labour Party leader, and one of the key platforms under his leadership was withdrawal from the EEC. It led to a split in the Labour Party in 1981, with Roy Jenkins, David Owen, Bill Rodgers and Shirley Williams leaving the party and setting up a new political party – the Social Democratic Party (SDP) – that supported continuing EEC membership. This party is examined under the Liberal Democrats below.

The 1983 General Election was really the first – and, to date, only – election where a major party campaigned for withdrawal from the EEC. The Labour Party election manifesto stated: 'We will negotiate a withdrawal from the EEC, which has drained our natural resources and destroyed our jobs'. Although clearly stated, the party was not overly strident in pushing this position. Regardless, the Labour Party suffered one of its worst ever election defeats in 1983. As a result, many of the policies proposed at that time were gradually reversed. Foot's successor, Neil Kinnock, gradually moved the party to a more positive position on the EC, to the extent that, by the 1989 elections to the European Parliament, Kinnock was able to claim that the Labour Party was more pro-EC than the Conservatives.

Yet such a claim masked huge divisions within the Labour Party. Some of these came to the fore during the debates on the Treaty of

European Union. At this time, MPs such as Tony Benn, Peter Shore and Bryan Gould, actively campaigned against the treaty. Gould went so far as to share a platform with Margaret Thatcher (who also campaigned against the treaty) to publicise a telephone hotline where people could express their support or opposition to the treaty. As a result of this action, Gould was effectively ostracised by the Labour Party. This was not over what he did but rather with whom he did it. His actions, and those of others who opposed the Treaty of European Union, led to accusations of an 'unholy alliance' of MPs and members of the House of Lords from all of the major parties who would do anything to derail the treaty. It was interesting that nobody commented on the unholy alliance of all three major party leaders and their front benches in their broad support for the treaty, with John Major, Neil Kinnock and Paddy Ashdown all campaigning for the treaty (although the last two wanted to include the Social Charter).

The subsequent leaderships of John Smith and Tony Blair have seen the Labour Party leadership adopt a still more enthusiastic position on EU membership. As Prime Minister, Blair has worked to shed the image of Britain as a reluctant European – although he was an anti-EEC campaigner in the 1970s! Blair signed up Britain to the Social Charter at the Amsterdam Treaty in 1997, and has been to the forefront in campaigning for enlargement, and for reform of both the Common Agricultural Policy and the budget. The majority of the Labour Party appears broadly supportive of his position over Europe. There are still those among the Labour Party ranks, however, who argue that Blair is not going far enough down the EU route. There are also those who argue he is going too far. There is merely a veneer of unity on the issue of Europe.

Among the opposition to the Blair platform, there is the likes of Austin Mitchell (MP for Grimsby). Mitchell is the Chairman of the Labour Euro-Safeguards Campaign, a body which has campaigned against signing up to the single currency, and has also opposed the draft EU constitution. Another Labour campaigner (although he is now standing as an independent Labour peer) who is against much of what Blair stands for on the EU is Lord Stoddart. He is a former Labour MP and is Chairman of the Campaign for an Independent Britain. As an MP, Stoddart campaigned for Britain not to join the

EEC, and has been most vigorous in his opposition to membership. The Campaign for an Independent Britain campaigns openly for British withdrawal from the EU. It is a cross-party organisation, which is chaired by Sir Richard Body and includes Teddy Taylor among the vice-presidents.

On the more EU-enthusiastic side, Lord Kinnock and Wayne David (MP for Caerphilly) are both members of the European Movement – UK. This organisation tries to promote and encourage greater British involvement in the European Union – it is also a cross-party organisation which contains Conservative and Liberal Democratic MPs. The European Movement – UK is actually part of the European Movement International, which tries to encourage all member states to participate more fully in EU affairs. Support for the euro and the draft EU constitution comes from this and other organisations. As with the Conservative Party, however, the number of Labour personnel who are quite so enthusiastic about the EU is a distinct minority.

For the vast majority of the Labour Party MPs, there is a tendency to toe the party line. This appears to be particularly true over Europe. The MPs follow the party leader. This has led to them being described as 'the soggy middle' and 'the ballast in the ship that wobbles'.[1] While not very complimentary towards these MPs, it is quite accurate. MPs of all parties can, and do, change their opinions on issues whether through pressure from the party whips or through personal experience. Even the former leader of the Labour Party, Neil Kinnock (a member of the European Movement, as noted above), was once opposed to EC membership, as was the current party leader, Tony Blair.

Liberal Democratic Party

The Liberal Democrats, and their predecessor parties (SDP-Liberal Alliance, and the Liberal Party), have been consistently pro-European in their outlook. Even going back to the original formation of the European Coal and Steel Community, it was the Liberal Party which urged membership. At that time, however, there were only six Liberal MPs, so their opinions were not treated with any degree of seriousness.

The Liberal Party was committed to joining the EEC in the 1970 General Election. When Parliament voted on British membership in 1971/72, not all Liberal MPs supported the move. One Liberal MP (Emlyn Hooson) voted against membership.

The issue of Europe came to the fore in the 1980s with the creation of the SDP. It was not just over Europe that members of this party disagreed with the Labour Party under Michael Foot, but Europe was important. The original party took thirteen Labour MPs and one Conservative MP in party defections. A strong pro-European line was developed by the leader, Roy Jenkins. This was a key factor in enabling the creation of the Alliance with the Liberal Party.

In the 1983 and the 1987 general elections, the Alliance polled around 25 per cent of the votes cast but gained very few seats. It was decided to rationalise the Alliance and merge the two parties – thus the Liberal Democratic Party was formed. Its first leader was Paddy Ashdown.

As noted above, the Liberal Democrats are broadly supportive of continued EU membership. They gave strong support to the signing of the Treaty of European Union – and, in doing so, kept the John Major Conservative government in power. Their support was given even though Major had negotiated opt-outs from both the social charter and the single currency. Despite this support for Major in the early 1990s, the Liberal Democrats are most likely to complain that Britain needs to engage further with the EU. They are, for the most part, committed to signing the draft EU constitution and to signing up to the euro, subject to a national referendum. While this is generally the official party line, however, not all MPs are fully supportive of it.

Nick Harvey (MP for North Devon) campaigned openly against the Treaty of European Union. He was the only Lib Dem MP in this position. While Harvey now claims to have moderated his Euroscepticism, he does not always toe the party line – although his promotion to the Lib Dem front benches may see a further moderation of opinion. He has even been joined by other Lib Dem MPs in voting against the party line on the issue of Europe. John Burnett (former MP for Torridge and West Devon) and Mike Hancock (MP for Portsmouth South) have voted against the party on EU issues more regularly than Harvey.

The minor parties

There is a number of smaller parties that also have important positions on the European Union. These are examined below.

UK Independence Party

The UK Independence Party (UKIP) was created in 1993. It is fundamentally opposed to continued British membership of the EU. This is its *raison d'être*. It wants Britain to withdraw from the European Union. All its other policy platforms are linked to this position. The party sees the EU as a burden on the British economy and on the British taxpayer. The perception of UKIP is that Britain would be far better off outside the EU than remaining as a member. Added to this, UKIP claims to be 'the only Party telling you the truth about the European Union'.[2]

In the 2004 elections to the European Parliament, the party campaigned on this platform and gained twelve MEPs. It made UKIP the fourth largest British party in the European Parliament. This was the peak of the party's relative success. Since then, it has been split. Its most prominent MEP, Robert Kilroy-Silk, attempted to take over the party leadership. He was unsuccessful in this and left UKIP to form his own party – Veritas. Consequently, in the 2005 General Election, the anti-EU vote was split between these two parties.

The problem for UKIP (and Veritas) is that the vast majority of the British people do not see EU membership as a key election issue (see chapter 9 on the EU and public opinion). This has made it very difficult for UKIP to have an electoral impact. The extent of this is demonstrated with the Hartlepool by-election of September 2004. UKIP claimed electoral success by coming third in the by-election, relegating the Conservative Party to fourth place. This 'success' was not maintained as UKIP fell to a distant fourth place in Hartlepool in the 2005 General Election.

Green Party

The Green Party is broadly supportive of membership of the European Union but it is also very critical of the EU. The Greens highlight many of the benefits and potential benefits of EU membership. Prominent here would be their support of the Kyoto protocols, and the way in which the EU has set targets for all member states to achieve with regard to reducing carbon emissions. Yet the Greens are also very guarded as to how they feel the EU should develop. For example, the party would like to see a fundamental overhaul of the Common Agricultural Policy. It is opposed to the introduction of the single currency across Europe, and is also against the development of a European superstate. Even its tentative support for an EU constitution was premised on the idea that it would be a 'green' constitution – putting the environment and people before corporate profit, and trying to make the EU more open and more accountable.

It has been through elections to the European Parliament that the Green Party has been able to have some sort of impact on British politics. In 1989, the Greens won 15 per cent of British votes cast in the elections to the European Parliament – but no MEPs. Currently, they have two MEPs, and they see this as a solid springboard to greater electoral success in the European Parliament as well as in other electoral contests across Britain.

Scottish Nationalist Party

The Scottish Nationalist Party (SNP) was originally opposed to EEC membership. The party saw it as some sort of capitalist club that had few, if any, benefits for an independent Scotland. Even during the 1975 referendum on EEC membership, the SNP campaigned for a 'No' vote.

It was not until after the 1983 General Election that the SNP started to revise its position on Europe. In many respects, its movement towards a more enthusiastic outlook on Europe has mirrored the movement of the Labour Party – although, arguably, the SNP has moved far more quickly towards a more pro-European outlook. By 1988, the SNP was campaigning for an independent Scotland within Europe.

Much of this move may be to do with the benefits that the Republic of Ireland received as a result of membership. The Irish economy has benefited from a huge level of investment via the structural funds. The SNP is of the opinion that an independent Scotland within the EU would receive similar levels of grants from the EU.

The SNP is not totally committed to everything that emanates from Europe, however. While there is a commitment to greater integration, the SNP is sometimes a little guarded in its support. For example, the SNP felt unable to support the proposed EU constitution. While there was support in principle for a constitution, the draft that was tabled did not gain SNP approval. One of the reasons for the lack of support stemmed from the Common Fisheries Policy. The SNP wants this particular competence to be returned to national governments. According to the SNP, the Scottish fishing industry is getting near to the point of collapse as a result of boats being tied up and total allowable catches (TACs) being reduced. The Scottish fishing fleet may be suffering more than those of the rest of Britain. Yet nothing is done about it in London.

The SNP believes that an independent Scotland should also sign up to the euro. The Scottish Nationalists have made a commitment to hold a referendum on this issue to let the Scottish people decide. Overall, the SNP has made a huge shift in its attitude to Europe. Just thirty years ago, no one could have imagined the degree of its support for the EU.

Plaid Cymru

Like their Scottish counterparts, the Welsh nationalists were originally opposed to EEC membership, and they also campaigned against membership in the 1975 referendum. As with the Scottish Nationalists, it was in the mid-1980s that Plaid Cymru started to become more enthusiastic about Europe. There was no sudden 'road to Damascus' change of position, however, and Plaid Cymru has gradually changed its position. Originally, it was opposed to membership. This then changed to tentative support for some sort of pan-European organisation. Much of this may have been as a result of the Thatcher government and its relative neglect of Wales. There was not outright support for Europe at this time; there was criticism of the Common Agricultural Policy and the Single European Act. Yet even this position has now changed to more wholesale support for the EU.

Today, Plaid Cymru is enthusiastic about EU membership. The EU is able to give much to Wales, and the Plaid Cymru politicians believe that Wales has much to give to Europe. There was, however, criticism of the EU when the number of Welsh MEPs was reduced from five to four in the 2004 elections to the European Parliament.

Plaid Cymru pointed out that Latvia – a country which is smaller than Wales – has greater representation in the European Parliament than Wales. Plaid Cymru would also like to see EU offices set up in Cardiff, just as there are in Edinburgh and in other capital cities around Europe.

Overall, Plaid Cymru is quite an enthusiastic supporter of the EU. As with most parties, this support is qualified. Plaid Cymru would like to see some reform to some of the EU policies, such as, the Common Agricultural Policy. Today, Plaid Cymru sees the EU as a useful avenue in which to promote Wales.

Northern Ireland parties
Politics in Northern Ireland is phenomenally complex, and the added dimension of the EU does not make things any easier. Many issues may be divided upon sectarian lines. As with mainland Britain, however, Europe does not sit comfortably across the political parties.

For example, the two main Unionist parties – the Democratic Unionists (DUP) and the Ulster Unionists (UUP) – are not overly enthusiastic about the EU. The UUP has not campaigned for withdrawal whereas, in the past, the DUP perceived the EU as a means of by which Roman Catholicism and the papacy could extend their influence across Europe. It is hardly surprising that the DUP has stated that it would like Britain to withdraw. This opposition to the EU did not stop the DUP from putting up candidates for the elections to the European Parliament, however. Over the last few years, the DUP position has moderated. While still not very enthusiastic about the EU – it is opposed to the euro and to the draft EU constitution – the DUP has been successful in campaigning to improve Northern Ireland's position in Europe. This includes things such as achieving Objective 2 status for structural funds. Like the DUP, the UUP has also campaigned against the draft constitution and against Britain joining the euro. Both parties are committed to furthering Ulster's (and Britain's) interests within the EU.

On the nationalist side of the fence, the Social Democratic and Labour Party (SDLP) has been quite enthusiastic about membership of the EU. The SDLP is probably the strongest supporter of EU membership in Northern Ireland. The party sees it as a useful tool by which the problems in Northern Ireland may be resolved. It has seen the euro introduced in the Republic of Ireland and would like the same for Northern Ireland. In fact, the SDLP adopted a rather interesting position for the elections to the European Parliament in 2004 where it campaigned for a dual currency in Northern Ireland (the pound sterling and the euro) until Britain made a decision in a referendum. The SDLP has also given guarded support to the draft EU constitution. The party considers it a useful document but with some work still needed on it.

Sinn Fein, on the other hand, has been opposed to EU membership. Currently, however, it is more enthusiastic about the EU but opposed to greater integration. The focus of Sinn Fein is upon both Northern Ireland and the Republic of Ireland. Thus, it highlights opposition to the Common Foreign and Security Policy because it may threaten Ireland's neutrality. The party was also opposed to Ireland signing up to the euro as it could result in surrender of economic sovereignty. Sinn Fein would now prefer to see Northern Ireland sign up to the euro (as the Republic is now using the currency) because there would then be a single currency in use across the whole of Ireland. Sinn Fein is also opposed to the draft constitution. While streamlining the EU is supported by the party, the proposed draft constitution does not meet all Sinn Fein's aims or expectations.

Today, all four of the major parties in Northern Ireland are committed to participation in the EU. Their degrees of commitment are variable. The SDLP is the only party to have been supportive of membership since the 1970s. The other three parties are seeking to gain from EU membership in an attempt to further their own domestic agendas. In the case of Sinn Fein, the agenda is for a united Ireland. Both the Unionist parties, on the other hand, wish to keep Ulster as part of the United Kingdom and feel this aim can be best achieved through engagement with the EU.

••

✓ What you should have learned from reading this chapter

- The major parties all have internal divisions on the issue of the EU. Some of these are glossed over by the parties. Not all MPs are willing to 'toe the line' of their party leaderships.

- Individual MPs, including some prominent politicians, such as Tony Blair, often change their minds on the issue of Europe.

- Most British political parties have changed their positions on the issue of Europe. Only the Liberal Democrats (and the SDLP in Northern Ireland) have been consistent supporters of membership.

- Of the smaller political parties, UKIP and Veritas both campaign for British withdrawal from the EU. These are the best known of the anti-EU parties.

- The smaller political parties in Scotland, Wales and Northern Ireland all try to use the EU to further their own domestic agendas.

🔎 Glossary of key terms

Collectivity This term is used to describe collective decision making by the British Cabinet. Once a decision has been made by the Cabinet, all members must support the decision publicly, even if they have private doubts. It is only in very exceptional circumstances that collective decision-making is suspended.

Free vote This is where 'whipping' of votes is suspended (see Three-line whip). MPs vote according to their consciences. Free votes are often used for contentious non-partisan legislation.

Minority government In this circumstance, a governing party does not have an absolute majority of seats in the House of Commons. Where this happens a party can either form a coalition with one or more of the other parties, or 'go it alone' and form a minority government.

Three-line whip The 'whipping' of legislation is used to compel MPs to follow the party line. A three-line whip is the strongest degree of whipping, where attendance and following the party line are considered 'essential'. A one-line whip is the weakest, where attendance and following the party line are 'requested'.

Tory Gaullist A Conservative Party MP (or supporter) who believes that Britain should be in the EU but that national interests should override those of the EU. This follows the line of the former French President, Charles de Gaulle, who always put French interests ahead of those of Europe.

❓ Likely examination questions

Why is Europe such a divisive issue for British political parties?

All the major political parties claim to be pro-European, yet their perceptions of Europe are significantly different. Why is this? What is meant by the term 'pro-European'?

'The European Union is one of the most divisive subjects in British politics but has never been, nor will ever be, an election issue.' Evaluate this statement.

Helpful websites

All the British political parties have their own websites. It is possible to access these and find old manifestos as well as current policy positions on the EU. The three main parties are: www.conservatives.com, www.labour.org.uk and www.libdems.org.uk. The Scottish and Welsh nationalists can be found at www.snp.org.uk and www.plaidcymru.org.uk respectively. UKIP's web page is www.ukip.org, while the Green Party can be found at www.greenparty.org.uk. The Northern Ireland parties mentioned in this chapter can each be found at www.dup.org.uk, www.uup.org.uk, www.sdlp.org.ie and www.sinnfein.ie.

Other organisations that draw support from MPs include the Campaign for an Independent Britain, which can be found at www.cibhq.co.uk/index.htm, the European Movement (www.euromove.org.uk/), and the Labour Euro-Safeguards Campaign (www.lesc.org.uk).

Suggestions for further reading

N. Ashford, 'The Political Parties' in S. George (ed.), *Britain and the European Community: The Politics of Semi-Detachment* (Clarendon Press, 1992) pp. 119–48.

K. Johansson and T. Raunio, 'Regulating Europarties', *Party Politics,* vol. 11, no. 5 (2005) pp. 515–34.

A. Jones, 'Parties, Ideologies and Issues: the Case of the European Community' in L. Robins, H. Blackmore and R. Pyper (eds), *Britain's Changing Party System* (Leicester University Press, 1994) pp. 75–92.

J. Turner, *The Tories and Europe* (Manchester University Press, 2000).

CHAPTER 9

Reluctant Europeans – Public Opinion on the European Union

Contents

Overview

There are many reasons why Britain has been perceived to be 'reluctant' about participating fully and enthusiastically in the European Union. One has been public opinion. British public opinion on the issue of Europe has fluctuated from being relatively enthusiastic to outright hostility. The one time that the British public was asked about EEC membership, however, a comfortable majority in favour was returned. What is also interesting is that many other countries within the European Union have also returned less-than-favourable opinion polls about membership – and some countries have even defeated referendums on European issues. Yet, for some reason, it is the British public that is portrayed as being reluctant and even opposed to EU membership. Having said this, what is also interesting is that the British public appears to be among the least well informed of all EU citizens.

Key issues to be covered in this chapter:

- British public opinion on the European Union
- Pressure group activity in Britain on the issue of Europe
- How pressure groups are able to lobby the European Union
- Public opinion on the European Union in other member states
- Turnout for the elections to the European Parliament

British public opinion on the European Union

What is interesting to note about British public opinion is that so very little appears to be known about Europe. In the media – and in particular in the tabloid newspapers – the portrayal of Europeans is often derogatory. Anything about Germany, for example, is likely to have reference to World War II – even football matches between England and Germany may evoke references to 1966 (when England beat West Germany to win the football World Cup) and to the war. This is anything but helpful when trying to move on to nurture any form of positive relationship with our European neighbours.

Lack of knowledge about Europe and the EU is not new. A survey was taken in 1971 before Britain joined the EEC. The question put to members of the public was to name the members of the **Common Market**. By using the phrase 'Common Market' there was no hint as to what countries could be involved – there was no prompt about Europe. The answers are detailed in Table 9.1. While it was promising to see that the majority of those surveyed could, indeed, name most of the six member states at that time, it was somewhat more disconcerting to see some of the other responses, including South Africa and Israel.

France, West Germany and Belgium were the most identified of the member states. Unsurprisingly, Luxembourg was identified by less than half of the respondents. This could be attributed to the size of the country.

Since joining the then EEC, the British public has been subject to the *Eurobarometer* survey. This takes snapshots of public opinion on a range of issues linked to Europe, with the same or similar questions being asked of the British and European publics. Yet, apart from these surveys, British public opinion has been tested only once on the issue of European membership. This was the referendum in June 1975.

The referendum, which was touched upon in an historical context in chapter 2, was fought beyond party lines. Thus, there was no official party guidance from the major parties on how to cast their votes. Members of the public, however, were given booklets explaining both the case for and the case against continued membership of the EEC, as well as the government's position on renegotiating the terms of entry. The result of the referendum is detailed in Table 9.2.

Table 9.1 Survey of members of the Common Market (1971)[1]

Identify the members of the Common Market (%)

France	91
West Germany	77
Belgium	72
Holland	64
Italy	57
Luxembourg	43
Switzerland	21
Norway	17
America	7
South Africa	4
Russia	4
Israel	2

Table 9.2 British referendum on EEC membership (6 June 1975)

	Votes cast	Percentage of votes
Yes	17,375,309	67.2
No	8,480,805	32.8

Turnout: 64.5%

This was a convincing result in favour of membership. Other opinion polls at that time had predicted a much closer result, and some even forecast a 'No' vote.

Since the referendum, there has been much talk as to the extent of dislike of Europe in Britain. Much of this may be attributed to apocryphal tales. These are often exacerbated by stories in the media of Brussels banning the British sausage or compelling donkeys to wear nappies while working on British beaches. Yet there is a knock-on effect from these stories. *Eurobarometer* surveys suggest that people seem to accept that there is more than a grain of truth in these tales. In the 'Executive Summary of the National Report on the UK' (2002), it was noted that: 'The UK generally has a low level of interest in the European Union which is not aided by their television viewing habits and the editorial attitude of some of the more widely read papers.'[2] Despite this rather pessimistic perspective on British interest in the EU, the *Eurobarometer* surveys have come up with some rather startling information. Some of the questions and responses are presented in Tables 9.3 and 9.4. What they show is a rather contradictory set of attitudes in Britain.

Over the last ten years, for the most part *Eurobarometer* has found that more people in Britain think that EU membership is a good thing rather than a bad thing. There was a tie in 2002 and 2004 between those who thought that it was a good thing and those who thought it was a bad thing. This positive result must be tempered by the number of people who responded either 'Neither good nor bad' and 'Don't know'. Anywhere between a third and a half of respondents gave such a reply.

To complicate matters further, there appears to be a feeling over the same time period that Britain has not really benefited from EU membership. There are two exceptional years: 2002, where 36 per cent responded favourably in that Britain had benefited from EU membership, whereas only 35 per cent felt otherwise (although this must be tempered by the 29 per cent who did not know); and 1998 where 40 per cent felt there was a benefit from membership, compared to 39 per cent against (with 21 per cent responding 'don't know'). In every other year, the negative responses outscored the positives – the biggest gap being 19 per cent in 2000. The number of those responding 'don't know' has fluctuated between a fifth and a third of respondents.

Table 9.3 Is Britain's membership of the European Union a good thing? (%)[3]

Year	Good thing	Bad thing	Neither	Don't know
2005	36	27	28	9
2004	29	29	29	13
2003	30	25	31	14
2002	32	32	21	15
2001	29	24	27	20
2000	25	24	29	22
1999	31	23	26	20
1998	41	19	30	10
1997	36	26	*	*
1996	35	25	*	*

* Data not availble

The level of 'don't know' responses across both of these survey questions is more than a little disconcerting, bearing in mind that Britain joined the organisation over thirty years ago. A lack of knowledge about Britain benefiting from EU membership might be expected. The question is rather stark, giving only 'Yes' or 'No' options for respondents. It could be considered difficult to measure how Britain might (or might not) benefit from EU membership. The first question with the 'Neither good nor bad' option gives the respondents the opportunity to sit on the fence – which almost a third of respondents have duly done. It is impossible to extrapolate as to whether or not this is an informed opinion, or whether respondents have responded in such a manner because they do not wish to seem ignorant. It might be interesting (or frightening, depending upon your perspective) to rerun the opinion poll to name the member states of the European Union. With twenty-five members, it is unlikely that the

Table 9.4 Has the United Kingdom benefited from EU membership? (%)[4]

Year	Yes	No	Don't know
2005	40	42	18
2004	30	47	23
2003	32	44	24
2002	36	35	29
2001	29	38	33
2000	25	44	31
1999	31	37	32
1998	40	39	21
1997	36	42	22
1996	38	43	19

average person in the street would be able to name all them. It is unlikely, however, that the United States, Israel and South Africa would be included in the responses.

Pressure groups and the European Union

Where we might expect to see more informed opinion on the issue of Europe is in the activity of pressure groups. What is often interesting here is the extent to which the information being peddled by these organisations is accurate. Regardless of the truth of the information, those involved in pressure-group activity tend to be people who have a keen interest in the subject – either in support of, or against, whatever aspect of Europe is being discussed.

Within Britain, it is note worthy that the anti-European pressure groups are more numerous and more active than the pro-European groups (see Table 9.5, although the lists are by no means exhaustive).

Table 9.5 Pro- and anti-EU pressure groups in Britain

Pro-EU Pressure Groups	Anti-EU Pressure Groups
• Britain in Europe (defunct as of August 2005)	• British Weights and Measures Association
• Centre for European Reform	• Bruges Group
• Conservative Group for Europe	• Business for Sterling
• European Atlantic Group	• Campaign Against Euro-Federalism
• European Movement	• Campaign Alliance for the Rights of the People
• Pro-Euro Pro-Britain	• Campaign for an Independent Britain
• The Federal Trust	• Congress for Democracy
	• Conservatives Against a Federal Europe
	• Democracy Movement
	• European Foundation
	• Free Britain
	• Free Europe
	• Freedom Association
	• Global Britain
	• Labour Euro-Safeguards Campaign
	• Magna Carta Society
	• New Alliance
	• Open Europe

Table 9.5 (continued)

Pro-EU Pressure Groups	Anti-EU Pressure Groups
	• The European Alliance of EU-Critical Movements (formerly The European Anti-Maastricht Alliance)
	• Youth for a Free Europe

Some of these pressure groups were mentioned in chapter 8 with regard to their links with MPs and political parties. Many of these groups operate quite happily without such connections, however. Some groups feel that it may harm their points of view to be too closely connected with either a political party or particular MPs. Such concerns were expressed by campaigners against the euro in the 2001 General Election when the Conservative Party leader, William Hague, campaigned with a timer showing how much time was left until Britain lost the pound. Anti-euro campaigners felt that if Hague lost the election, people might be resigned to losing the pound as well.

Among all the different pressure groups, those that are less enthusiastic about Europe appear more likely to have some connections with MPs, former MPs, or members of the House of Lords. One such group is the Campaign for an Independent Britain which was mentioned in chapter 8.

What needs to be noted in Table 9.5 is that a very crude distinction has been made about these pressure groups. If they stand on any sort of anti-EU platform, then they are listed as anti-EU. Yet it could be possible for a group to be against joining the euro but still in favour of EU membership. Bill Cash (MP for Stone) once made such a complaint about being pro- or anti-European on the issue of the Treaty of European Union:

> We are told that the choice is between accepting Maastricht [Treaty of European Union] or repudiating the European Community as a

whole. To be anti-Maastricht is said to be anti-European. This is an insular argument, which assumes that the only question for the British is whether they should be in or out . . . Any argument based on this unreal alternative is untenable and anti-Community.[5]

Those organisations listed under the anti-EU label cover a wide range of issues. For example, the British Weights and Measures Association (BWMA) simply wants Britain to retain imperial measurements (miles, yards, pints, ounces, etc.) rather than being compelled to move to metrication (metres, kilometres, kilograms, litres, etc.). As a result of joining the EEC, metrication can be forced on the British people through the need to standardise systems across all the member states. The BWMA will do whatever it can to resist such a move.

Other anti-European groups focus far more on a broad range of issues. The BWMA is very much a single-issue organisation. The Bruges Group and the Campaign for an Independent Britain have a far broader remits on the issue of Britain and the European Union.

The Bruges Group was established in 1989 after a speech made by Margaret Thatcher (British prime minister at the time) to the College of Europe in Bruges. Thatcher pointed out that Britain had 'rolled back the frontiers of the State' and that she did not want them reimposed at a European level. Thus, the Bruges Group campaigns for less state/EU involvement in British affairs. Ultimately, the Bruges Group is running a campaign against the establishment of a European state and is keen for Britain to disengage from the EU. Its members include Baroness Thatcher, Iain Duncan Smith (Conservative MP and former party leader), John Redwood (Conservative MP), Frank Field (Labour MP) and Nigel Farage (UKIP MEP).

The Campaign for an Independent Britain has a broader appeal than does the Bruges Group. Although the Bruges Group contains supporters who are not members of the Conservative Party, the vast majority of prominent members belong to the party. The Campaign for an Independent Britain does not have such close ties to a particular party. As noted in chapter 8, the chairman of the organisation is Lord Stoddard (a former Labour peer), the president is Sir Richard Body (Conservative) and the vice-presidents include Sir Teddy Taylor (Conservative). Like the Bruges Group, the Campaign for an Independent Britain works towards Britain leaving the EU.

The Campaign for an Independent Britain was formed in 1976 as the Safeguard Britain Campaign. It changed to become the British Anti-Common Market Campaign (in 1983) before adopting its current moniker. It is considered to be one of the groups to the forefront of the campaign to get Britain to withdraw from the EU.

On the more EU-enthusiastic side, there is the European Movement. As with the anti-EU groups mentioned above, the European Movement is a cross-party organisation. More accurately, it is a pan-European movement. Collectively, it was founded in 1948 (and was chaired by Sir Winston Churchill) with the aim of preventing further war in Europe. The British branch was formed a year later. The British 'branch' should be called, more accurately, the European Movement – UK. Within the European Movement – UK, there are prominent politicians, including Kenneth Clarke (Conservative MP), Lord Kinnock (Labour peer) and Baroness Williams (Liberal Democrat peer). The organisation provides a lot of information about the positive aspects of membership, including a section entitled 'What Europe has ever done for us?' as well as providing a list of other pro-European organisations.

How do pressure groups lobby the European Union?

When thinking about pressure groups, most people tend to focus on domestic politics and on how pressure groups access central or local government. Yet more and more pressure groups are now shifting their focus to the EU.

It could be argued that, within the EU, the role of pressure groups has, to some extent, become institutionalised. Within the structures of the EU, there is a specific body which encompasses pressure groups – the **Economic and Social Committee** (see chapter 3). The drawback here is that national governments select the membership for their national delegation. Thus, it is likely that delegates in the Economic and Social Committee are considered 'acceptable' to their national governments. A further drawback to the Economic and Social Committee is that it is an advisory body. Although it has expertise and is likely to be consulted, there is no obligation on other EU institutions to follow the advice of the Economic and Social Committee.

Table 9.6 British pressure group delegates in the Economic and Social Committee

Member	Organisation
Richard Adams	Consultant in social, environmental and ethical business
Anne Davison	Foodaware/Fair Trade Foundation
Claire Donnelly	Northern Ireland Tourist Industry Confederation
Rose D'Sa	Consultant in EU, Commonwealth and International Law/Consultant in legal education/distance learning
Maureen O'Neill	Royal Bank of Scotland Centre for the Older Person's Agenda
Sukhdev Sharma	Migration Policy Group/Runnymede Trust
John Simpson	Economics consultant/adviser

For all the many pressure groups excluded from the Economic and Social Committee, other points of access to the EU are required. The reality is that a pressure group would be out to target either the Commission or the European Parliament. The Council of Ministers is more likely to be a national target rather than an EU one – a pressure group would be more likely to lobby its own national government rather than the government of another country.

One of the interesting things is the extent of pressure group activity in the EU. There are hundreds upon hundreds of 'recognised' organisations. This means that the Commission acknowledges the knowledge, specialisation or contribution that could be made by these 'recognised' groups. These groups are listed in the Commission's own database.[6] This is, again, almost a case of institutionalised lobbying. But it appears to work. The Commission actively encourages such pressure-group activity. Many of these groups have huge resources and degrees of specialisation that may be lacking within the formal EU institutions. Many of them are also conglomerations of national pressure groups.

With the range of different groups in operation, what often happens is that cross-national links are established. An example of such linkages can be seen with the trade unions. In Britain, for example, there is the TUC (Trades Union Congress). This body could lobby the EU on a range of matters related to the welfare of employees. It helps that a third of Economic and Social Committee members represent workers, organisations. As part of the European Trade Union Confederation (ETUC), however, they have a far more powerful collective voice.

Many pressure groups also set up offices in Brussels. This is not dissimilar to the actions of the different tiers of subnational government in Britain which have done the same (see chapter 5). Basically it means that a permanent office is on hand to respond to any given issues or concerns that may arise. Thereafter, the lobbying processes are not too dissimilar to those used in national politics. The key difference is that the focus tends to be on the Commission rather than on politicians

Public opinion across the European Union

With public opinion in Britain being somewhat less than enthusiastic for the EU, it is little wonder that Britain retains the label 'reluctant European'. When compared with public opinion in other EU member states, however, some of this apparent British 'reluctance' is a myth that may be questioned.

From polls in the spring of each year between 2000 and 2005, it is fairly obvious that the British public comes last of the EU-15 when asked if membership of the EU is a good thing (see Table 9.7). Austria, Finland and Sweden regularly come close to Britain's responses – and, pre-2004, these three states were the most recent countries to join. At the other end of the scale, the country that polled the highest for membership being a 'good thing' was Luxembourg. Other enthusiastic member states included Ireland and the Netherlands. It is rather surprising that the Dutch felt that membership of the EU was a 'good thing' when they voted against the draft constitution of the EU.

While the British response for support of EU membership is not very high – ranging between 25 and 36 per cent, the EU average is not overly spectacular. In fact, in half of the surveys covered, a minority

Table 9.7 Membership of the European Union is a good thing (EU-15) (%)[7]

State	2005	2004	2003	2002	2001	2000
Belgium	67	57	67	58	54	62
Denmark	59	54	63	60	48	53
Germany	58	45	59	52	45	41
Greece	56	71	61	64	57	61
Spain	66	64	62	66	57	67
France	51	43	50	47	49	49
Ireland	75	71	67	78	72	75
Italy	56	54	64	69	57	60
Luxembourg	80	75	85	81	72	75
Netherlands	77	64	73	71	63	73
Austria	37	30	34	37	34	33
Portugal	61	55	61	62	57	64
Finland	45	46	42	40	36	40
Sweden	44	37	41	38	33	34
United Kingdom	36	29	30	32	29	25
EU-15 average	55	48	54	53	48	49

of the EU population thought that EU membership was a good thing. The alternative responses were 'bad thing', 'neither' or 'don't know', as can be seen earlier in this chapter, in Table 9.3.

Where the question focuses upon whether the respondent's country benefits from EU membership, you might expect that

Table 9.8 My country benefits from EU membership (EU-15) (%)[8]

State	2005	2004	2003	2002	2001	2000
Belgium	69	58	57	58	55	60
Denmark	70	64	70	68	61	65
Germany	50	39	45	43	39	37
Greece	69	82	74	72	69	75
Spain	69	69	62	63	54	66
France	53	46	50	49	47	49
Ireland	87	80	77	86	83	86
Italy	52	49	52	62	49	51
Luxembourg	72	69	74	70	66	69
Netherlands	67	55	65	67	63	65
Austria	41	38	41	40	38	34
Portugal	67	66	68	69	68	71
Finland	50	46	46	41	38	42
Sweden	36	27	31	29	27	26
United Kingdom	40	30	32	36	29	25
EU-15 average	54	47	50	51	45	47

support would fall in most member states. There is no such clear pattern (see Table 9.8). What is interesting is that in only one of the polls does Britain come last (2000). In every other year, Sweden comes out below Britain – but it is the only country to do so. The country which consistently topped the poll was Ireland.

Across both sets of surveys, Britain, Sweden and Austria are consistently the least enthusiastic member states when it comes to EU membership. It is interesting to note that all the larger member states (Germany, France, Britain and Italy) tend to return around the 50 per cent marker or less in most of the surveys. The country that consistently topped the polls in acknowledging benefits from the EU was Ireland.

Where you might expect to see a high degree of support is in the new member states. Their responses are in Table 9.9. What is interesting here is that the new member states reduce the average score in membership as a good thing by 1 per cent. Conversely, they raised the benefit return by the same amount.

It is also interesting to note the returns on various referendums on European issues. While the results of the membership referendums

Table 9.9 New member states responses (2005) (%)[9]		
State	**Support membership**	**My country benefits from membership**
Czech Republic	49	56
Estonia	48	58
Cyprus	43	41
Latvia	42	57
Lithuania	59	72
Hungary	42	47
Malta	40	53
Poland	53	62
Slovenia	49	62
Slovakia	54	63
EU-25 average	54	55

Table 9.10 Referendum results on EU issues

Issue	State	Date	Yes (%)	No (%)
Treaty of European Union	Denmark	June 1992	49	51
		May 1993	57	43
	France	Sept. 1992	51	49
Treaty of Nice	Ireland	June 2001	46	54
		Oct. 2002	63	37
Euro	Sweden	Sept. 2003	43	57
Draft Constitution	Spain	Feb. 2005	77	23
	France	May 2005	45	55
	Netherlands	June 2005	38	62
	Luxembourg	July 2005	57	43

in the applicant states are detailed in Table 9.12, Table 9.10 gives the results from a variety of referendums held in EC/EU member states. Those included are just a sample. It is interesting to note that both Denmark and Ireland have returned 'No' votes in specific referendums, and have been compelled to hold them again!

Notice that four of these referendums have returned 'No' votes – Denmark on the Treaty of European Union, Ireland on the Treaty of Nice, and France and the Netherlands on the draft EU constitution. Both Denmark and Ireland were compelled to hold their respective referendums a second time, with the Commission instructing the Irish to 'get the right result'! To date, no such pressure has yet been brought to bear on the French or the Dutch. This may be a consequence of two member states returning negative votes.

Many of the votes have been very close affairs – most notably the French 'Yes' and Danish 'No' votes for the Treaty of European Union. Conversely, Spanish enthusiasm for the draft constitution was surprisingly high.

Even with all these 'No' votes on European issues from a number of member states – including two founder members – the European project marches on. It has been suggested by some cynics that the European Union refuses to accept any negative votes, and that it will continue to rerun any referendum until a 'Yes' vote is achieved. It is hardly surprising that enthusiasm for the EU struggles to stay above the 50 per cent level.

Turnout for European parliamentary elections

It has often been suggested that the real enthusiasm, or rather lack of it, can be seen in the **turnout** for elections to the European Parliament. These elections were first held in June 1979, and have been held on a fixed five-year term thereafter. Thus, at the time of writing, there have been six elections.

Belgium has always had an exceptionally good turnout for its elections to the European Parliament. Every single one has had a turnout of over 90 per cent. This is because there is **compulsory voting** in Belgium. Other countries with high turnouts include Italy and Luxembourg. Britain has always been criticised for having the poorest turnout for the elections to the European Parliament. This is not always the case, as can be seen in Table 9.11. Britain has, however, languished close to the bottom of the turnout table in every election, at least until 2004.

In four of the five elections between 1979 and 1999, Britain had the lowest turnout – the exception was in 1994 when it was third from bottom. In 1994, both Portugal and the Netherlands had turnouts below that of the United Kingdom – although both were only marginally so. In 2004, Britain recorded its highest turnout for elections to the European Parliament (38.9 per cent).

In 2004, the overall average turnout for the European Union fell to an all time low of 44.2 per cent. Much of this has been attributed to the poor turnouts in many of the new member states that joined in 2004. While Malta and Cyprus recorded very high turnouts, none of the East European countries broke the 50 per cent turnout barrier. The average across all ten new member states was 28.7 per cent, while the old EU-15 recorded 47.7 per cent. This was still a fall in turnout for the older member states (which would have been to an all-time

Table 9.11 Turnout for elections to the European Parliament

Country	1979	1984	1989	1994	1999	2004
Belgium	91.6	92.2	90.7	90.7	90.0	90.8
France	60.7	56.7	48.7	52.7	47.0	42.8
(West) Germany	65.7	56.8	62.4	60.0	45.2	43.0
Italy	85.5	83.9	81.5	74.8	70.8	73.1
Luxembourg	88.9	87.0	87.4	88.5	85.8	90.0
Netherlands	57.8	50.5	47.2	36.0	29.9	39.3
Denmark	47.1	52.3	46.1	52.9	50.4	47.9
Ireland	63.6	47.6	68.3	44.0	50.5	59.7
United Kingdom	*31.6*	*32.6*	*36.2*	*36.4*	*24.0*	*38.9*
Greece	78.6[a]	77.2	79.9	71.2	70.2	63.4
Portugal	–	72.2[b]	51.1	35.5	40.4	38.6
Spain	–	68.9[b]	54.8	59.1	64.4	45.1
Austria	–	–	–	67.7[d]	49.0	42.4
Finland	–	–	–	60.3[d]	30.1	39.4
Sweden	–	–	–	41.6[c]	38.3	37.8
Cyprus	–	–	–	–	–	71.2
Czech Republic	–	–	–	–	–	28.3
Estonia	–	–	–	–	–	26.8
Hungary	–	–	–	–	–	38.5
Latvia	–	–	–	–	–	41.3

Table 9.11 (continued)

Country	1979	1984	1989	1994	1999	2004
Lithuania	–	–	–	–	–	48.4
Malta	–	–	–	–	–	82.4
Poland	–	–	–	–	–	20.9
Slovakia	–	–	–	–	–	17.0
Slovenia	–	-	–	–	–	28.3
EU average	63.0	61.0	58.5	56.8	49.4	44.2

– no elections to the European Parliament as the country was not a member of the organisation
[a] election was held in 1981
[b] election was held in 1987
[c] election was held in 1995
[d] election was held in 1996

low). Turnouts in France, Germany and Spain fell to just above 40 per cent. Conversely, turnouts in Britain, the Netherlands and Finland rose markedly to just below 40 per cent. Surprisingly, Britain and Luxembourg both recorded their highest ever levels of turnout in the 2004 elections. Luxembourg recorded a turnout of 90 per cent. Regardless of the 'good news' about improved turnouts in Britain and Luxembourg, the turnouts for the elections to the European Parliament have decreased from one election to the next. It had been hoped that, with the parliament gaining new powers via the Treaty of European Union, people might take a greater interest. This has not been the case. National issues are still seen to be of far greater importance than those of the EU.

The reasons given for the poor turnouts in the new East European member states appear to revolve around dissatisfaction with the European Union. There had been a perception that the EU was going to pour monies into these states, and to build up their economies and

Table 9.12 Referendums on EU membership 2003

Country	Yes vote (%)	Turnout (%)
Czech Republic	77.3	55.2
Estonia	66.9	63.0
Hungary	83.8	45.6
Latvia	67.7	72.5
Lithuania	91.1	63.4
Malta	53.6	91.0
Poland	77.5	58.9
Slovakia	92.5	52.2
Slovenia	89.6	60.3

their agricultural sectors in particular. These expectations had not been met. In fact, across the new member states, there was a high degree of disillusionment with the EU. The problem is that this disillusionment was not necessarily a result of EU actions. The governments of these countries sold the idea of membership to their respective peoples on the idea that the EU was going to be some sort of cash cow. They did nothing to suggest otherwise. There was little or no attempt by the governments to dampen down expectations. Those who opposed EU membership, and who suggested that the expectations of funding were little more than a pipe dream, were dismissed. In retrospect, those foreboders of doom and gloom appeared to be more in touch with reality than the campaigners for joining the EU.

A quick comparison on electoral turnout for the new member states in Table 9.11 can be made with Table 9.12. The latter table shows the turnout and percentage in favour of membership in national referendums held in all the then applicant states. Of the ten that joined, only Cyprus did not hold a referendum on membership.

In each referendum, there was a sizeable majority in favour of membership. The closest result was in Malta, where just over 50 per cent of the population voted 'Yes' on a turnout of over 90 per cent! Slovakia polled the largest percentage support for membership (92.5 per cent), with a turnout of just over 50 per cent. Hungary and Slovakia had the lowest turnouts in their referendums on joining the EU. For Slovakia, the 52.2 per cent in the referendum was significantly more than the 17 per cent for the elections to the European Parliament just one year later. Even the Polish turnout plummeted from 58.9 per cent to 20 per cent. The Hungarian turnout was only marginally lower than the turnout in the referendum (45.6 per cent down to 38.5 per cent in the elections).

Conclusion

What seems to be apparent across much of the EU is that the public is not overly enthusiastic about Europe. The 'No' votes for the draft EU constitution in France and the Netherlands appear symptomatic of this disillusionment. Even though Spain and Luxembourg returned 'Yes' votes for the draft constitution in their respective referendums (and, in the case of Spain, with 77 per cent of voters saying 'Yes'), it seems as if the EU institutions have failed to engage with the European people.

José Manuel Barroso, the President of the European Commission, appears eager to reinvigorate the constitution. To be able to do this successfully, however, there will be a need for the European Union to reconnect with the people. Expectations as to what the EU can do have been built up but not always realised. Faults are always found – particularly in the Eurosceptic press. What the EU needs to do is to promote and publicise its success stories. It also needs to educate the people about what the EU does. Such a scheme must start in the schools of Europe. Schoolchildren across much of the EU have knowledge of the EU that would put most British adults to shame. It is this type of information campaign that is needed. There must be no rose-tinted spectacles, however: successes and failures must be included. At the same time, the perceived railroading of Europe towards a United States of Europe needs to stop. It is a waste of time, effort and money to go down that route when the vast majority of the

European public does not know what is involved, and therefore wants little or nothing to do with such a project.

· ·

✔ What you should have learnt from reading this chapter

- The British public is not overly enthusiastic about EU membership, and is unclear about the extent by which Britain benefits from EU membership

- The degree of knowledge in the UK about the EU is very low.

- Most other EU states are somewhat more enthusiastic about EU membership although the newer member states are already raising concerns

- Turnouts for elections to the European Parliament have been decreasing from one election to the next. The United Kingdom is among the member states that have the lowest turnouts.

🔎 Glossary of key terms

Common Market A term used to describe the original European Economic Community. There was always the suggestion of a single market, in name if not in deed.

Compulsory voting Some countries, such as Belgium, require all voters to cast their ballots in an election. Failure to do so can result in a fine or even imprisonment.

Economic and Social Committee An unelected body which draws in people from different aspects of economic and social life: employers, employees and pressure groups. It is a consultative body and its opinions are not binding.

Turnout The percentage of the voting population which casts (or spoils) its ballot on polling day.

❓ Likely examination questions

Why does the issue of the European Union conjure up such apathy within Britain?

Electoral turnout for European parliamentary elections in Britain is lower than that for local government. What can be done to turn this around?

Why is the European Union so popular in member states such as Ireland?

Helpful websites

Plug any of the pressure groups' names into a search engine and you ought to be able to access their websites. Some of the key groups are:
The Campaign for an Independent Britain – www.bullen.demon.co.uk
The Bruges Group – www.brugesgroup.com
The European Movement – UK – www.euromove.org.uk

Eurobarometer surveys can be found at
www.gesis.org/en/data_service/eurobarometer/index.htm

The European Commission database of consultative bodies and civil society organisations can be found at europa.eu.int/comm/civil_society/coneccs/index_en.htm. These databases also provide access to the different groups' web pages as well. The European Trade Union Confederation web page is at www.etuc.org/.

Suggestions for further reading

D. Butler and U. Kitzinger, *The 1975 Referendum* (Macmillan, 1976).

W. Cash, *Europe: The Crunch* (Duckworth, 1992).

J. Greenwood and M. Aspinall (eds), *Collective Action in the European Union: Interests and the New Politics of Associability* (Routledge, 1998).

J. Greenwood, *Interest Representation in the European Union* (Palgrave, 2003).

R. Jowell and G. Hoinville (eds), *Britain into Europe: Public Opinion and the EEC 1961–75* (Croom Helm, 1976).

R. Pedler (ed.), *European Union lobbying: Changes in the arena* (Palgrave, 2002).

CHAPTER 10

Conclusion – Is Britain Still the 'Reluctant European'?

Contents

Overview

This book has repeatedly referred to the idea that Britain is labelled a 'reluctant European'. Britain was 'reluctant' for refusing to join in the 1950s, as well as being 'reluctant' ever since joining. Yet how appropriate is this label? The problem is that the phrase 'reluctant European' means different things to different people. It may well be that the phrase 'reluctant European' is wholly inappropriate to describe Britain's relationship with the European Union in the twenty-first century. Even the phrase 'awkward partner' may not be that useful. There are deep divisions within British politics over the issue of Europe. It is somewhat inaccurate to describe the British as being (collectively) 'reluctant Europeans'. To do so drowns out the Euroenthusiasts across the country. The negatives of membership of the European Union are always highlighted in the media; the positives are ignored. Perhaps this is why Britain is still considered to be the 'reluctant European'.

Key issues to be covered in this chapter

- What is a 'reluctant European'?
- Why Britain might still be perceived to be a 'reluctant European'
- The case against Britain being a 'reluctant European'
- Are any other EU states 'reluctant Europeans'?

What is a 'reluctant European'?

In chapter 2, the issue of what a 'reluctant European' was raised. What became apparent was that there were several different types of reluctant European. At different times, Britain could be considered as being 'reluctant' depending upon the definition being used. For example, countries that do not wish to apply for membership or have turned down membership could easily be considered to be 'reluctant Europeans'. This would encompass countries such as Norway and Switzerland. Under such a definition of 'reluctant European' Britain could be considered as such only from the formation of the European Coal and Steel Community (ECSC) until the first application for membership in 1961. Thereafter, with Britain applying for membership repeatedly, and then joining the then European Economic Community (EEC), Britain does not conform to such a narrow definition of 'reluctant European' – and has not conformed to such a definition for over forty years!

An alternative extreme definition of Europe is to go far beyond simply the European Union and its forebears. This definition would encompass organisations such as the **European Free Trade Association (EFTA)** and the **North Atlantic Treaty Organisation (NATO)**. These are all 'European' organisations (although NATO also includes some non-European members such as the United States and Canada). Britain has participated in such organisations – and continues to participate in those for which it is eligible for membership. This idea of Europe goes far beyond EU membership. Some EU members, such as Ireland, are not members of NATO. Other European countries do not belong to any of them (for example, Switzerland). It could be argued that, by not participating in these European organisations, that a country is indeed a 'reluctant European'. Thus, Ireland's policy of neutrality means that the Irish government will not join a military organisation such as NATO. Arguably, by not joining in this collective defence pact for Europe, the Irish are 'reluctant Europeans'.

These two extremes – of not joining the European Union and of not joining other (non-EU) European organisations – are very narrow. The reality is that, while the term 'reluctant European' could be applied to these extremes, it is now more readily applied to the way in which European states participate in the EU.

Box 10.1 What is a 'reluctant European'?

Europe is 'the source of deep divisions within parties. This is because, although England has always been a part of Europe and is deeply European in its culture, its language, its institutions, its religion and its politics, the national identity first of England, and then of Great Britain and the United Kingdom, has generally been formed in opposition to "Europe", or at least to some suitably frightening manifestation of Europe. It has often been convenient to make Europe the "Other" against which the peculiar qualities of Englishness and Britishness are defined. One of the "Metric Martyrs" (small shopkeepers fined in 2001 for refusing to introduce metric weights and measures in their shops) declared after the court hearing: "I am British; I am *not* European", as though the one necessarily excluded the other. The belief that they could be, and should be, exclusive still fuels political debate.'[1]

'There were several reasons for Britain's reputation for awkwardness: domestic political constraints on the positions that British Governments could adopt; the real problems for the British economy in adjusting to membership, especially the problem of Britain's contributions to the common budget; an awkwardness on the part of British negotiators in handling the terminology of political debate that had developed amongst the original members; and an instinct of many leading political figures to look first to the United States for partnership.'[2]

There is a range of different things to consider when using the label 'reluctant European'. Is the focus upon signing treaties and the extent to which member states commit themselves to these treaties? Alternatively, it could be about the extent to which member states implement regulations and directives that are issued by the EU. A third approach could be about the way in which member states' representatives conduct themselves at EU summits or at meetings of the Council of Ministers.

The case for Britain being a 'reluctant European'

There are many reasons why Britain is still labelled the 'reluctant European'. As noted earlier in this chapter (and in chapter 2), the historical arguments still apply. Britain refused to join the original coal and steel community as well as the EEC. Britain was clearly 'reluctant' to join. There were many valid reasons why Britain refused. The knock-on effect, however, was that Britain had no input into the formative years of the organisation. As a result, when Britain did eventually join, the modus operandi of the organisation was significantly different from the way in which politics operated in the United Kingdom. The consequence of this was that successive British prime ministers found themselves at odds with, or even isolated from, the rest of the organisation. Thus Britain seemed to be a reluctant partner.

A clear example of this was Margaret Thatcher and Britain's budgetary contributions. Thatcher argued that Britain paid too much into the budget and that too much of the budget was spent on agriculture. Thus, she demanded that Britain required a rebate to enable monies to be directed to aspects of the British economy that were in far greater need of support than agriculture. Yet there is an argument that the whole idea behind the EEC was to enable the more agrarian economies to benefit from the more industrialised ones. Now this was probably appropriate in the 1950s and 1960s (when the EEC was barely formed). It was probably less appropriate by the 1980s (and even less so today). This was how the EEC was originally structured, however, and Britain, as a non-member, had no input into this policy area.

What makes Britain's situation within the EU rather worse is the extent of non-EU relations. Most EU member states have some form of relationship with states outside the Union. The French have their former colonies, as do the Belgians, Dutch and Italians. The Poles have a close relationship with the Ukraine. All the former communist states have some form of relationship with modern Russia. For Britain, it is far more complicated. There is the Commonwealth (which has members from every continent) and the 'special relationship' with the United States. It is the latter that makes Europe suspicious of British motives. It seems that whenever there is a crisis, Britain takes its lead from the United States rather than from the European Union. In the 1960s, when Britain's independent nuclear deterrent failed, it was to the US that Britain turned for a replacement. Britain's American-made Polaris trident missiles were replaced by American Trident missiles in the 1980s. When there is trouble in

---

Box 10.2 Europe or America?

'While it remains true that the choice between Europe and America for Britain can never be an exclusive one, since both European and American influence on British politics is deep and lasting, there is a question of priority for the future, and whether if the United States continues its pursuit of American primacy, the long-established commitment by the British state to its strategic alliance with the United States will be sustainable. This policy appeared to reach breaking point at the time of the Iraq war, and it raised doubts as to whether any future British government would be able to support the United States in the way the Blair government has managed to do . . .

Growing criticism of the policy of the United States highlighted the importance of Europe as an alternative pole to the United States in the world order. In a multi-polar world the EU will have a central place, and it is for this reason that the EU continues to grow in importance in British politics . . .

The Blair Government is in any case wedded to the idea of Britain as a bridge between Europe and America, and Ministers have constantly asserted the importance of Britain being at the heart of Europe.'[3]

---

the Middle East – be it over Suez, Israel, Iraq or Iran – Britain looks to the United States for guidance rather than to Europe. It was not surprising that the former French president, Charles de Gaulle, refused Britain entry into the EEC because he felt it was a Trojan horse by which the United States could interfere in European affairs. Some may argue that little has changed. Hence, Britain is reluctant to be a member of the European Union.

One consistent theme concerning Britain as a 'reluctant European' has been the way in which successive British governments have complained about membership, and have organised opt-outs from different policy areas. The Heath government negotiated the terms of entry but these were then renegotiated by Harold Wilson's government – much to the consternation of the EEC. The results were then put to a national referendum. At this stage, it could have been argued that perhaps Britain might actually commit itself more wholeheartedly to the European project. It was not to be. Thatcher wanted 'our money back'. She was accused of 'handbagging' her European partners. Added to this, she resisted any moves to develop a social platform within the European Community or to permit the free movement of people around Europe. She also negotiated the British rebate in 1984. This rebate – which was to redress the excessive spending on the CAP by a refund for Britain – has become a British 'sacred cow'. No government is willing to surrender this rebate. To do so would be political suicide, risking the wrath of the British tabloid press. In 2006, however, Blair signalled a willingness to see the British rebate reduced, but only a little.

Thatcher's successor, John Major, negotiated '**opt-outs**' at the Maastricht summit where the Treaty of European Union was drawn up. These 'opt-outs' were the final steps in the process towards the single currency as well as to the Social Chapter of the treaty. The 'opt-out' of not signing up to the single currency has been maintained by Tony Blair. All this suggests that Britain is still not fully committed to the European project.

Another area where British reluctance has been perceived is over the proposed EU constitution. The Blair government promised a referendum on the proposal but has since reneged on this promise. Arguably, the 'No' votes in France and the Netherlands have left the proposed constitution dead in the water. This did not stop Luxembourg from holding its referendum. The possibility of a British 'Yes' vote (though most unlikely) would have put the proposed EU constitution back on track. The refusal to even attempt to hold the referendum was a signal to the EU that Britain was anything but fully supportive of the constitution.

A final aspect where Britain is most clearly seen as a 'reluctant European' is in the British media – particularly the tabloid press. All the British tabloids, and most of the quality dailies, are far from supportive of EU membership. Headlines such as 'Up yours, Delors', and fabricated stories, such as donkeys having to wear nappies on British beaches or banning of the British sausage, are vitriolic in their sentiment against Europe, bordering on the xenophobic. These papers influence public opinion about Europe (the overall figures can be seen in the range of tables in chapter 9). As long as this remains the position of the tabloids then Britain will remain the 'reluctant European'.

Regardless of which definition is used (as detailed earlier in the chapter), Britain is a 'reluctant European'. The refusal to join in the early years was followed by complaints and opt-outs after membership. Successive British governments have dragged their heels on a range of policy initiatives. It could even be argued that Britain's reluctance has held back the development of the European Union as a whole.

The case against Britain being a 'reluctant European'

While the case for Britain still being labelled a 'reluctant European' is relatively straightforward, the case against may appear less clear-cut but is no less compelling. The perception of Britain complaining about various EU policies is not necessarily that it is opposed to them but rather that the British government would like them to be thought out more clearly.

In some respects, Britain can be seen as being at the forefront of the development of the European Union. Successive British governments have been the most enthusiastic supporters of enlargement. Even at the time of writing, Britain is the strongest supporter of Turkish membership. The argument is that the benefits of EU membership should not be felt by a small minority of states. Rather, they should be extended to any state that meets the criteria to join. Thus, for the British government, as long as Turkey (or any other applicant state) meets the ***acquis communautaire*** then it should be eligible to join. It is interesting to note that other member states, including some of the founder members, are far less enthusiastic about widening membership.

This position of support for broadening the European Union is not an isolated example of how Britain has played a key role in its development. In particular, Britain's current and previous prime ministers have attempted to move Britain closer to the centre of the EU. This was phenomenally difficult for John Major. Before Major took over as party leader, the Conservative Party was split over the issue of Europe – and remains so to this day. Yet, as prime minister, John Major played a key role in moulding the Treaty of European Union. He will be remembered for negotiating the 'opt-outs' for Britain. Yet he ought also to be remembered for the development of the European

Ombudsman system, as well as the concept of **subsidiarity**. While these concepts may be relatively unknown to the British public, the Ombudsman system has introduced a greater degree of account-ability in the Union. Arguably, it can be seen as a small step in com-bating the idea of a **democratic deficit**. Similarly, Major saw subsidiarity as taking some of the powers away from the central EU and returning them to national governments – again, part of the fight against a democratic deficit. Other member states saw subsidiarity as possibly taking powers away from either the Union or from central governments and returning them to regional or local governments (whichever was the most appropriate tier).

Upon gaining the premiership of Britain, Tony Blair immediately signed up the country to the Social Charter (thus renouncing one of the 'opt-outs' that John Major had negotiated). This was completed at the Treaty of Amsterdam. Added to this, Blair has also been keen to enlarge the European Union and to develop its international role. Thus, there has been a lot of enthusiasm for the European **Rapid Reaction Force**. Blair sees this as an organisation that would work alongside NATO rather than supplanting NATO. It would provide the EU with a small military role – probably as peacekeepers – in any regional conflicts near, or within, Europe.

The Blair government has also been eager to reform some of the common policies of the European Union. Some of this was touched upon in chapter 4 but is worth brief mention again. Paramount for Britain is reform of the Common Agricultural Policy (CAP) and the budget. The two go hand in hand, and reform of one depends on reform of the other. Blair wants to see European finances used far more effectively. This means less spending on agriculture and more on development and encouraging enterprise. If there are steps towards significant reform of the EU budget and the CAP, it appears that he might even be willing to surrender the British rebate.

Thus, in sum, all this goes to show that the British are not 'reluct-ant Europeans'. It is important to acknowledge that there are prob-lems, but Britain is not alone in experiencing them. At times, Britain is capable of being a constructive and keen member of the European Union. It may even be the case that other EU partners are actually more deserving of the label.

Are any other EU members 'reluctant Europeans'?

It is possible to argue that almost every member state could be considered a 'reluctant European'. The eight East European states that joined in 2004 are already complaining that they are being deprived of their rightful subsidies via the CAP and the structural funds. It became so bad in Poland, for example, that the people elected anti-EU parties in the elections to the European Parliament only one month after joining! Added to this, Cyprus is already digging in its heels over the proposed Turkish membership. Bear in mind that, in a national referendum on the reunification of Cyprus (after Cyprus had joined the EU), it was the Greek side that voted 'No', not the Turkish side of the island!

The Danes, the Irish, the Dutch and the French have all at one time or another voted against the Union in national referendums (see Table 9.10). It took the Danes two attempts to ratify the Treaty of European Union and the Irish two attempts to ratify the Treaty of Nice. The Dutch and the French voted against the proposed EU constitution. Each of those votes slowed down or prevented further development of the organisation. Yet, for some reason, none of them was labelled a 'reluctant European'.

When there are any proposed reforms to the European Union – be they institutional or policy based – there are outcries from some member states. Even simple things, such as a reduction in milk subsidies, saw some member states negotiating preferential treatment to delay the cuts in subsidies – but only for themselves. The culprits? France, Ireland and Spain. Some proposed reforms have been agreed but do not take effect until 2014. This is the year in which all the states that joined in 2004 become eligible for 100 per cent of their subsidies via the CAP, structural funds, and so on. Unsurprisingly, this has caused consternation among the newer member states. All round, it is a case of national interest being placed ahead of the collective EU interest.

For countries such as France, reform of the common policies or the budget should not be examined in isolation. The British rebate, or *cheque Britannique*, is a huge problem. The British economy is now more than strong enough to cope without the rebate. Thus, from a French position (although they are not alone here), any substantial reform of the CAP or the budget will not commence until the British rebate is ended. Jacques Chirac (President of France) was rather adept at playing this card when Tony Blair proposed some reform to the CAP and the budget under the British presidency of the Council of Ministers. For him, and no doubt for France, no reforms could take place until the *cheque Britannique* was given up.

The list of examples of member states acting in a manner that does not befit committed European partners could go on and on. Every member state has been guilty of such actions. Britain is the only member to be tarred with the label 'reluctant European'. It may well be the case that such a label is no longer appropriate.

Conclusion – if Britain is not reluctant, then how can the relationship be labelled?

The problem here is that, if the British government questions any proposals from the European Union, the immediate response is that Britain is being reluctant. Yet this reluctance may actually serve the EU well, especially if the proposed policies have been poorly thought out. Being able to question a proposal is not necessarily being reluctant. It could be being cautious or careful. Such an approach is more often than not healthy for a democracy. Bearing in mind that the EU is often accused of suffering from a democratic deficit, such caution (or care) may actually be quite appropriate.

The problem for Britain in particular is that any member state that appears to be dragging its feet over EU policies is going to be condemned for doing so. Successive British governments (but especially those under the Thatcher premiership) appeared to do whatever they could to slow down the integration processes, if not the entire development of the Union. Other countries may have shared British misgivings but none did so as vocally as the British government. It was as if the British government was a lightning conductor for dissatisfaction. Consequently, the label 'reluctant European' may have been appropriate.

Yet, even allowing for Thatcherite scepticism of the European project, there appears little stomach for Britain to leave the Union. It is only the extremes of British politics – on both left and right – that advocate withdrawal. The reality is that most Britons accept

---

Box 10.3 Is Britain really reluctant?

'On the one hand, the claim is made that Britain is a "good European", implementing EU legislation and actively working with and through EU institutions; on the other hand, there is the persistent suggestion that Britain cannot be dictated to by the EU and should both challenge and thwart the "threat" posed by Brussels. These differences serve to generate highly contentious politics around the growing influence of the EU in the everyday life of the UK.'[4]

---

the fact of membership. The problem is over the speed and direction of the European Union. Here it is not reluctance but, rather, caution.

There is a growing sentiment that the European Union is going too far, and definitely too quickly, down an integrationist route. Most Britons would like the process to slow down. There is a fear that the body could disintegrate if all members are forced into some sort of United States of Europe. And Britain is not alone in expressing such sentiment – although only Britain's voice seems to be heard. There is not reluctance about the European project, rather caution. The process should be more evolutionary than revolutionary. People need to get used to the current developments within the EU before moving on to the next. This is best exemplified over the proposed EU constitution. The French and Dutch 'No' votes should have struck a note of caution within the Union, especially taken alongside some the fact that member states are now refusing to hold referendums on this issue (most notably Britain and Poland).

Perhaps we should stop talking about the 'reluctant European' or even the 'awkward partner'. There are positive aspects to Britain's relationship with the European Union as well as negative ones. The same applies to all member states. Britain, though, appears to be the member state that suggests to the EU that the integrationist programme needs to be slowed down. This is not a sign of reluctance. In the future, it is most likely that a British government will go down this path, with the support of the British population . . . but not yet. There needs to be a note of caution, and this seems to be provided by

Britain. Britain is not a 'reluctant European'. A far better way to describe the relationship is that Britain is a 'cautious European'.

....

✔ What should you have learnt from reading this chapter

- There is a number of different explanations of the phrase 'reluctant European'. It could be applied to a country not wanting to join the European Union or to a member which does not participate fully in the Union.

- Britain has been branded the 'reluctant European', yet the actions of other member states have been such that they are just as deserving of the label.

- The positive aspects of British membership are rarely highlighted in the media.

- The label 'reluctant European' may no longer be appropriate for Britain. Phrases such as the 'cautious European' may be far more appropriate.

🔍 Glossary of key terms

Acquis communautaire This is the package of treaties and legislation which has already been passed by the European Union that any new member states must accept as part of joining it.

Democratic deficit This is a difficult term to explain although, at a basic level, it suggests a lack of democracy. This could be because there is little or no electoral accountability, or that there is a lack of transparency in the decision-making process – which again suggests a lack of accountability to the people.

European Free Trade Association (EFTA) This was a body set up to counteract the EEC. The emphasis was upon free trade, particularly in industrial goods. There was to be no surrender of sovereignty.

North Atlantic Treaty Organisation (NATO) This is a defence pact that was signed by West European and North American states in 1948. Originally it was to protect Western Europe from a possible Soviet invasion. With the demise of the Soviet Union, many East European states have joined NATO. It now acts as an international policeforce and peacekeeper.

Ombudsman This loosely translates as a grievance person. The Ombudsman investigates maladministration – policies that have been implemented badly or inappropriately. The system acknowledges that people need an avenue for complaint in such circumstances.

Opt-out An opt-out can be negotiated by any member state with regard to a policy that may adversely affect national interests. Thus, Britain Denmark and Sweden opted out of the euro.

Rapid Reaction Force The Rapid Reaction Force is the EU's military response unit. It comes under the Common Foreign and Security Policy.
Subsidiarity This is the process of devolving decision-making down to the most appropriate tier of government. At its most basic level, the aim of subsidiarity was to take decision-making away from the EU and return it to national governments. Some aspects of subsidiarity could see decision-making being devolved to regional or local government.

Likely examination questions

'Britain is no longer the "reluctant European".' Discuss.

Britain looks to both the United States and the European Union to assist in solving global problems. The remedies proposed by each side are of the wholly incompatible, however. How could future British governments resolve this situation?

'Britain's future would be best served outside of the EU.' Discuss.

Helpful websites

The website Free Britain at www.freebritain.co.uk gives a comprehensive overview of all Eurosceptic websites. The Foreign Policy Centre also has a number of articles on Britain and the EU at www.fpc.org.uk/topics/europe/.

Suggestions for further reading

A. Gamble, *Between Europe and America: The Future of British Politics* (Palgrave, 2003).

S. George, *An Awkward Partner: Britain in the European Community* (Oxford University Press, 1994) 2nd edition.

M. Smith, 'Britain, Europe and the World' in P. Dunleavy, R. Heffernan, P. Cowley and C. Hay (eds), *Developments in British Politics 8* (Palgrave, 2006) pp. 159–73.

References

Chapter 1

1. L. Robins, 'Britain and the European Community: Twenty Years of Not Knowing' in B. Jones and L. Robins (eds), *Two Decades in British Politics* (Manchester University Press, 1992) p. 243.

Chapter 2

1. S. Burgess and G. Edwards, 'The Six Plus One: British Policy-making and the Question of European Economic Integration, 1955', *International Affairs*, vol. 64 no. 3 (1988) pp. 393–413.
2. For an excellent overview of the entire negotiation process, see U. Kitzinger, *Diplomacy and Persuasion: how Britain joined the Common Market* (Thames and Hudson, 1973).

Chapter 3

1. *What the Ombudsman can Do for You. The Ombudsman: a Guide for Citizens*, European Communities (2002). This guide can be found at www.euro-ombudsman.eu.int/guide/pdf/en/guide_en.pdf.

Chapter 4

1. The table is developed from *Agricultural Situation in the EU: 2003 Report* (European Commission, Directorate-General for Agriculture). This is cited at europa.eu.int/comm/agriculture/agrista/2003/ table_ en/ 341.pdf.
2. europa.eu.int/comm/competition/state_aid/overview.

Chapter 5

1. Developed from www.parliament.uk/parliamentary_committees/euro-pean_ scrutiny/european_scrutiny_members.cfm.
2. Source: www.parliament.uk/parliamentary_committees/parliamen-tary_committees 26. cfm.

3. www.wales.gov.uk/keypubassemeuropeancomm2/index-e.htm.
4. Source: www.detini.gov.uk/cgi-bin/get_story?fold=106&site=
   6&parent=85&prevpage=&stid=233&openbus=6&golive=31-10-
   2003.

Chapter 6

1. Developed from www.epp-ed.eu/Members/en/default.asp.

Chapter 7

1. S. Nello, *The European Union: Economics, Policies and History* (McGraw-Hill, 2005) p. 382.

Chapter 8

1. A. Jones, 'Parties, Ideologies and Issues: the Case of the European Community' in L. Robins, H. Blackmore and R. Pyper (eds), *Britain's Changing Party System* (Leicester University Press, 1994) p. 83.
2. www.independence.org.uk.

Chapter 9

1. Developed from a Social and Community Planning Research (SCPR) poll cited in R. Jowell and G. Hoinville (eds), *Britain into Europe: Public Opinion and the EEC 1961–75* (Croom Helm, 1976) p. 68.
2. *Eurobarometer 'Special Bureaux'(2002) EB56.3 – National Report – United Kingdom* Executive summary p. 11.
3. Source: *Eurobarometer* surveys.
4. Source: *Eurobarometer* surveys.
5. W. Cash, *Europe: The Crunch* (Duckworth, 1992) p. 14.
6. See europa.eu.int/comm./civil_society/coneccs/index_en.htm for the lists.
7. Source: *Eurobarometer* surveys.
8. Source: *Eurobarometer* surveys.
9. Source: *Eurobarometer* No. 63.4 (2005).

Chapter 10

1. A. Gamble, *Between Europe and America: The Future of British Politics* (Palgrave, 2003) p. 108.
2. S. George, *An Awkward Partner: Britain in the European Community* (Oxford University Press, 1994) 2nd edition, p. 255.
3. A. Gamble, *Between Europe and America: The Future of British Politics* (Palgrave, 2003) pp. 223–24.
4. M. Smith, 'Britain, Europe and the World' in P. Dunleavy, R. Heffernan, P. Cowley and C. Hay (eds), *Developments in British Politics 8* (Palgrave, 2006) pp. 160–1.

Index

Bold indicates that the term is defined